WHAT'S RIGHT WITH FEMINISM

Elaine Storkey

GRAND RAPIDS, MICHIGAN
WILLIAM B. EERDMANS PUBLISHING COMPANY

Copyright © Elaine Storkey 1985

First published in Great Britain 1985 by SPCK

This edition published 1986 through special arrangement with SPCK by
William B. Eerdmans Publishing Company
255 Jefferson Ave. S.E., Grand Rapids, Mich. 49503

Edited by Tim Dean
This book was first published in the United Kingdom in conjunction with
Third Way, an evangelical monthly magazine that seeks to provide a bibli-
cal perspective on politics, social ethics, and cultural affairs. Further in-
formation may be obtained from *Third Way,* 37 Elm Road, New Malden,
Surrey KT3 3HB, England.

Library of Congress Cataloging-in-Publication Data

Storkey, Elaine, 1943-
What's right with feminism.

Includes index.
1. Feminism.   2. Feminism — Religious aspects —
Christianity.   3. Women in Christianity.   I. Title.
HQ1154.S685   1986   305.4′2   85-29170

ISBN 0-8028-0177-3

Contents

Introduction

The explosion of women on to the radical scene in the 1960s was regarded as part of the baggage of the age, part of the intense reflection and rejection of so many traditional social values. The media, anxious as ever for sensation, enjoyed the caricatures they created and, greedy for amusement, fanned the flame of male chauvinism, stereotyping all women who took a serious interest in the issues as bra-burners. Then as the counter-culture slowly melted away, and its leaders and gurus, in more conventional dress now, found less radical ways of expressing their belief in an alternative society, so the aggression, outrage and anger of the Women's Liberation Movement seemed also to evaporate into a reluctant acceptance that oppression was here to stay. Consequently, radical feminists withdrew into the security of their communes, and society reasserted the *status quo,* trying to forget they had ever happened. Successive governments concentrated on unemployment and inflation, bringing old answers to old questions. In a country with three and a half million unemployed, who has the luxury to consider the arguments of a handful of intellectual women?

Yet this is only half the story. In fact no society ever 'returns' to a former state. Insinuations, accusations and denouncements once made on such a large scale and so vociferously cannot easily be forgotten or dismissed. For whatever reason, some people have listened. Where arguments were persuasive, with or without the help of the media, then those who had no other direction found their sympathies roused and a long-term cause to espouse. Those with discontented lives, themselves often the victims of male harshness or prejudice, felt the warmth of identity and a recognition of their own situation. Those ready to attach themselves to anything disapproved of by the conservative orthodoxy had yet another pie for their thumbs, and those merely carried away by the attitudes of their peers found interesting slogans to mouth, and actions to copy. But further afield the issues have been brought into the consciousness of many other serious-minded members of the community who are able to recognize the injustice of a situation, and who can see through the ridiculousness of the media presentation to the deep, underlying issues. Many who would not in any clear way have identified themselves with the women's movement nevertheless accepted that in many areas their case was substantiated and that change must come. What could not be achieved for the women of that generation can be started for the next, and as research exposes area after area of inequality, so education programmes begin the desocialization of sex roles. Everything, from early reading schemes to sexual behaviour, from careers advice to ideas of parenthood, comes under scrutiny with similar findings thrown up: we are handing on misleading stereotypes about the capabilities, appropriate education, and moral obligations of the different sexes. We are therefore now seeing the *quiet* revolution, as offensive material is weeded out and replaced, but one more far-reaching than anything which took place in the heady days of discovery and consciousness-raising. It is in the middle of this quiet revolution where most women are called upon to make some response in their own lives to the ideas of the feminists that many are confused, and with traditional values still apparently upheld, but shifting beneath them, unable to say where they stand. Not least among these are Christian women, those single, married, with children, those contemplating marriage, those with adult families, those committed to a career, those in student circles. As a Christian, a woman, a worker, a wife and a mother, I have written this with them in mind. I am grateful to my Open University students and colleagues for stimulating ideas and sharpening my own perspective in this area. Diane Bailey contributed more than she realized. So did the women who attended my courses at Calvin and Covenant Colleges. I have also been grateful for the sisterly support of Kathy Keay, Miriam Sampson and Margaret Old who offered valuable comments to the first draft and Sue Fishwick who helped with typing. During the last week of writing my parents, James and Anne Lively, helped us at home. To two people, however, very special thanks are due. Tim Dean urged me to write this book and supported it enthusiastically throughout, even when very ill with leukaemia, and Alan Storkey has been in the project at every stage, clarifying the text, typing the manuscript, preparing the index and loving the author.

PART ONE
THE FEMINIST CASE

Modern Western society, argue the feminists, unlike its pre-industrial counterpart, is a society in which women are dependent, manipulated, vulnerable, passive and exploited and men are dominant. Society is designed by men for men, and women are seen as functioning to uphold and support the male domination. Thus, woman's work, whether at home, in the factory, in the office or hospital echoes daily her total dependence upon the subordination to the man. In this section, then, I want to look at the description feminists give of women's exploitation at work, in the home, in the professions, educationally, before the law and in the Church, and glimpse at some of the contributing factors behind these. In the next section we shall look more in depth at what they see to be the root causes of the inequalities.

1: Women at Work

'The problem of unemployment would be solved if all the women who did not need to work gave up their jobs for the men.'

I have heard this posited as a serious suggestion more than once, which indicates not only a worrying naivety about the causes of unemployment, but also considerable misunderstanding about the reasons why women work or the part they play in the economy as a whole. It betrays also an unexamined assumption that 'work' is done by men, and that women, by implication, ought to be doing something else. From the outset then we need to examine the role of women at work and the kinds of jobs they do. We shall then be in a better position to discuss discrimination against women in the labour market.

Some statistics

Figures for the British labour market are compiled by taking those in employment along with those registered as unemployed and receiving benefit.[1] On these figures women have made up about 40 per cent of the work force since the mid-seventies. Nor are these predominantly single women. Between 1961 and 1981 the total number of people in the labour force increased by over two million: an increase entirely due to the number of married women taking up work or registered as looking for work. By the 1980s about 60 per cent of all married women were in paid employment, dropping only to 58 per cent among women of child-bearing and child-rearing age. Yet even this figure is a conservative estimate. Women who work in a private domestic capacity in other people's homes are rarely recorded in the official statistics. Nor do government figures recognize those women who are looking for jobs but are not eligible for unemployment benefit. As long ago as 1965 a Government Social Survey revealed that only 16 per cent of women had not done any paid work since marriage. All indications are that this figure has dropped very much more since then.

This movement of women into the labour force is not a phenomenon peculiar to Britain. Women's participation in employment has risen throughout the EEC. Both Denmark and France have a higher percentage than the UK of women who work outside the home. Similarly, in the US women now make up about 40 per cent of the work force. The increase in married women working there is particularly marked. It is estimated that in 1940 only 9 per cent of women with school-age children sought employment; by 1975 this had risen to 52 per cent. The percentage for women with pre-school children is now approaching 40 per cent.

What these figures show then is that women are not merely a 'fringe' element of the labour market. Nor is work outside the home incidental to most women's experience. In Britain more than ten million women (compared with fifteen million men) are in paid employment. Much of our economy depends heavily on women's labour. Yet even early in the 1980s of this enormous female work force almost three quarters were crowded into the distributive trades and service industries. (This marked a substantial increase since 1959 when only 58 per cent of women had been employed in these areas.) Similarly, of those in manufacturing over one half worked in only four industries: food, drink and tobacco, electrical engineering, textiles and clothing. So the increasing movement of women into paid employment has for the most part taken place within those industries already characterized by high female employment. Whole areas of work have been marked off specifically for women. In fact, from 1911 to 1979 women's share of skilled manual work almost halved, whereas their share of unskilled and lower paid jobs more than doubled. Yet again this is echoed in the United States, where one study showed that half of all working women were employed in just twenty-one of the 250 occupations listed by the US Bureau of the Census.[2] What was more, just five occupations: secretary, domestic worker, book-keeper, infant teacher and waitress accounted for a quarter of all employed women. It is easy to see, then, that the continuation of 'women's jobs' makes it easier for employers to justify the difference in wages given to men and women. The British Equal Pay Act stipulates equal pay for equal work, but if the only people carrying out a certain task are women they have no comparative man's wage to argue from.

To reinforce this argument it is often pointed out that as well as being crowded into a few sectors of employment women are also located in the lowest paid jobs in industry. Women comprise 90 per cent or more of all clerical workers, nurses, canteen assistants, store cashiers, cleaners, laundry workers, domestic assistants, but about the same proportion or more of all surgeons, solicitors, architects, bankers, consultants, engineers, senior civil servants, university professors, airline pilots, chartered accountants, managers, judges, etc, are men. Even in jobs where women make up the majority of employees they form only a minority of those in senior positions. Thus, in primary school teaching in the mid-seventies 78 per cent of the teachers were women, yet only 43 per cent of headships were occupied by women. In non-professional occupations the situation is even more unbalanced. In catering women account for 73 per cent of the total labour force, yet only 16 per cent of the managers. In clerical occupations, even though around 99 per cent of all typists, shorthand writers and ancillary secretaries are women they comprise only 14 per cent of office managers.

Equal pay?

It comes as no surprise therefore to learn that in 1982, twelve years after the Equal Pay Act was passed, and six years after it became legally enforceable, the average earnings of a full-time woman employee were two thirds that of the average man. If we were to take into account the much higher earnings of many employers, the vast majority of whom are men, the proportion would be even smaller. The General Household Survey in 1980 calculated that a woman with GCE 'A' levels earned on average less than a man with no qualifications. Of course almost half of all married women work part time, and it is in this area where the greatest inequalities occur. No job security, no pension rights, no holiday pay or sick leave and low hourly rates are features of many women's working experience. Sylvia Walby argued in 1983[3] that the reason unemployment rates among women were lower in the UK than in many EEC countries was that part-time workers worked under such poor conditions that they were particularly attractive to employers.

Many feminists insist that, far from improving the position of women at work, the Equal Pay Act and the Sex Discrimination Act have left some women in a worse situation. The era of the 'token woman' came into existence, where a woman was sure to be included in a short list or on a panel where the job in question could be suitably filled with either sex. But it did not open the door for employment equality. Moreover, instead of a gradual levelling of men's and women's wages, jobs were re-graded, supervisory posts introduced where previously there had been none, and wage differentials remained much as before. In *The Equality Report*[4] produced by the National Council for Civil Liberties, Jean Coussins tells of the firm which paid higher wages to male toilet attendants than to female toilet attendants on the grounds that 'a male toilet attendant had to approach the job from a labouring point of view and a female from the housekeeping point of view'.

Stereotypes and status symbols

The lower pay and lower promotion prospects are not the only features of women's work which attract attention, however. There is a strong argument that, especially in white collar jobs, women are often used to enhance the status of men. Just as the success of the male breadwinner a century ago could be measured in the size of his domestic staff, today the importance of the successful man can be indicated by the number of people he can put between himself and the public. This stands out very clearly in the National Health Service, for example, where the hospital consultant (usually a man) has junior doctors, nursing staff, secretaries and receptionists for patients to wade through before they can be admitted into his presence. Similarly, although for different reasons, a businessman can see his glory reflected in a retinue of attractive women, answering his telephone, typing his memos, filing his reports, answering his correspondence, making his coffee and soothing his nerves. 'Impossible man,' reads the advertisement, 'chaotic and demanding, wants unflappable, dedicated secretary, with a warm personality and sense of humour . . .'

In this climate, therefore, it is not surprising that some men who work with women see women's existence at work primarily in terms of being of service to themselves, and there are clearly more unpleasant aspects to this for a minority of women. For some men indeed this implies that the women should be available for any service the man requires, and sexual harrassment at work is becoming a recognized

8

problem. It is not particularly that this is a new phenomenon; it is more that women are now less prepared to accept this as a necessary feature of their work lives. Harrassment in fact takes many forms. It may be merely whistles and comments with sexual innuendo which are served up day by day from the men they work with. It may be bottom-slapping, thigh-pinching, being physically handled or stroked by particular men. It may even reach the form of sexual intimidation, persistent requests for dates or weekends away. Many women in all kinds of work have to endure the presence of female nude pin-ups, often covering a large area in some shared workplaces. Often new pin-ups are brought in and shared around the men in front of the women, who thus feel their own sexual privacy being violated and undermined. Yet women are made to feel 'prudish' or unreasonable if they protest. The problem is widespread. In a group of women I spoke to, all working in different locations and at different jobs, and coming together simply on an Open University course, no fewer than half claimed to have experienced unpleasant sexual overtones at work, and two out of thirty had left their jobs because of it. The ones who had not experienced harrassment were the ones who worked alongside men as equal colleagues, or who spoke of being with 'tolerant' or 'unusual' bosses. The fact that even their non-harrassment was explained in this way gives weight to the feminist argument that the sphere of work is still *defined* by men, even though women now make up such a large force within it. Part of the definition of their work for some women is that men behave in this way towards them, and they must accept it as a given. In some cases which reach the courts it is evident that the penalty for not complying with the demands of the male hierarchy can well be unfair dismissal for some women.

Training and job security
Two other considerations still remain in relation to women and work. The first concerns training. Although as long ago as 1964 the Industrial Training Act made training available to a wider number of people, it is argued that this has not substantially increased the woman's chances either in the job market or in promotion prospects. Training has not been available through government training centres, well provided

for, but in commercial colleges where little has been done to encourage women to look beyond the usual clerical work. As far as day-release is concerned the picture is the same. In 1973 under 11 per cent of women in employment were on day release, against almost 40 per cent of men. A similar trend was evidenced in apprenticeships. 110 women held apprenticeships to skilled craft occupations, compared with 112,000 men. Even by 1981 women represented 74 per cent of those studying hairdressing, but only 0.5 per cent of those in construction and welding.

The other consideration concerns job security and employment. We live in an age marked by insecurity of tenure and distanced decision-making. A lifetime's work may be prematurely terminated through a take-over. People whose whole life revolves around work in one small urban area of Britain, might find everything is altered by a set of decisions made by unknown people half a world away. In this climate job insecurity amongst women is the most marked. During the period 1974 to 1981 male unemployment in England and Wales rose around 300 per cent, an appalling figure. However, during the same period female unemployment rose 800 per cent. In a financial crisis or cut-back, those with least muscle are often the most expendable. The services of the odd cleaners, ward orderlies, the extra secretaries, a few nurses, girls on the check-out tills, part-time teachers, can most easily be dispensed with. At the same time, it is often the very cheapness of some of these services which prevents unemployment amongst women rising much more.

If this is an accurate representation of some of the inequalities experienced by women at work, the curious question is, why do they persist? With changes in the legal position of women at work, and an ever-increasing number of women entering the work force, why does it seem to many that equality is further away now than a decade ago? The answers given to this often reveal the different perspectives which are found in both the feminist and non-feminist camps. Is it that women are simply poorly unionized; that the male unions are more concerned to look after themselves, and that even in unions where women make up the majority of the membership they comprise only a tiny minority of its officials (see the CPSA for example)?[5] Is it because women in the end are temperamentally unsuited to work, and that this sphere is not their 'natural' domain? Is it that they are merely the pawns of a capitalist economy, seen as a 'reserve army of labour' to be called in and out of the labour market as the needs of the economy dictate? Is it that they have been so domesticated by a patriarchal society, that their own self-image and definition are couched in terms of keeping home? Is it that successive societies have failed to think in a contemporary way about the relevant role of women in their generation? Is it that Christians have been too ready to support the status quo of a male hierarchy without carefully examining their assumption in a biblical light? We shall begin to unpack these responses in more depth later in the book.

One issue we might briefly open up here, though, is that a key response focuses on how women's work is seen by men, and often by women themselves; in other words, on the ideology of work.

Why work?
The point most frequently made is that a woman works for pin money, for luxuries: a new car, better holidays, private education for her children. This may well be the experience of some women but for the large part the evidence questions it. Professional women are more likely to work because they are totally involved in their job, because their own understanding of themselves is wrapped up in their identity at work. Women who do work largely to supplement their husbands' wages do so increasingly from a sense of *necessity* rather than desire for luxury. Moreover many women only have one income: particularly the single, divorced and separated. Other allegations are that women see their work in terms of companionship, sociability, an escape from the boredom of the home. This may well be true again for some women, but it is equally true for some (and probably more) men. Then it is argued women work for social and family reasons; therefore they are more likely to take time off work to look after children, and are consequently unreliable employees. A brief look at the statistics, however, reveals that women's absence from work through 'sickness' and related causes is nevertheless much lower overall than that of men.

One point does remain substantial, however, and that is that women's work is still seen by both men and women as secondary to their domestic roles. It is suggested frequently that women arrange work round the family whereas men arrange their family lives around their work. To some extent this is true even of young single women, who often take jobs with marriage and family life as a long-term view and their job as an occupation before and after this period. So it is to this aspect of home, marriage and family life that we now turn for the next argument in the feminist case.

Notes

1. All statistics referring to the British labour force are taken from *Social Trends* 1983, the *Annual Abstract of Statistics* 1983, the *General Household Survey*, or *Department of Employment Gazette* April 1981.
2. Quoted in Francine D. Blau, 'Women in the Labour Force: An Overview' in J. Freeman (ed.) *Women: A Feminist Perspective* (California, Mayfield Publications, 1975), p. 221.
3. Sylvia Walby, 'Patriarchal Structures: the Case of Unemployment' in E. Gamarnikov (ed.) *et al, Gender, Class and Work* (Heinemann 1983) p. 160.
4. Jean Coussins, (ed.) *The Equality Report* NCCL, Kings Cross Rd, London, 1975.
5. Table quoted in *Women: Directory of Social Change.* Wildwood House, London, 1978. The USDAW with union membership as 54 per cent of the whole, has only five full-time women officials over against 147 men. CPSA with 65 per cent membership women has two women out of fifteen of its officials.

2: Wives and Mothers

The male breadwinner: the family centrepiece

Ninety per cent of men and women in Britain marry at least once; 80 per cent of all men and women have one or more children and live with them for eighteen years or more. Kinship and marriage therefore structure most people's domestic arrangements for much of their lives. Even so, census figures indicate that fewer than one sixth of all households in Britain contain a married couple with dependent children where the father only is employed and the mother is a full-time housewife. Yet still the idea of the 'male breadwinner' as the economic focus of the family persists. In fact, in many working-class families where wives work full time, the wife's wages might account for 40 per cent or more of the family income, and are thus essential to the family's economic survival. Interestingly, studies suggest that equality in decision-making between husband and wife is significantly greater here than in families where wives' earnings are lower than their husbands. This of course is interpreted by feminists as evidence that authority in the family is based more on an ideology of economic power than on Christian ideas of 'headship'. It is for this reason then, the argument goes, that the myth of the male breadwinner persists: it reinforces the domination of the husband and keeps the wife as theoretically 'dependent' even if this is not true in actuality.

The centrality of the man in marriage is therefore a popular theme. Just as the paid work a woman does is seen in relation to the family, the unpaid, non-domestic 'services' she renders echo this male centrality: 'Dorothy is the best wife any hard working writer ever had. She types all her husband's business letters and manuscripts, criticises his work and reads books for him. She is also a splendid cook and housekeeper and lively and amusing talker.'[1] Many wives help their husbands in their occupations and their leisure lives, entertaining business guests, making sandwiches for the cricket club, keeping an appointments diary, acting as a personal assistant, taking phone messages, handling callers, chauffeuring, answering correspondence. A wife will often 'take over' family duties of her husband too: remembering his parents'

13

birthdays, anniversaries, buying presents for brothers or
sisters, visiting grandmothers. Many a mum enjoys a Mothers'
Day card from her married son, yet despite the signature
knows it to have been bought by a busy daughter-in-law. As a
teacher in a theological college I receive carefully typed and
immaculately presented essays, yet know they are as much a
product of a wife's work as of her student husband. Unpaid
wifely labour, often given lovingly and unstintingly, continues
to be part of the picture of marriage today. The fact that it is
rarely reciprocated to the same degree indicates that the
husband's job, leisure, training, time and education is seen as
the valuable one, and that the wife is still seen predominantly
as his supporter. In many areas, even down to making meals,[2]
the wife's own tastes and interests are often voluntarily
disregarded so that the husband's preferences can be
followed. It is this same sacrificial, unpaid supportive role
which the archetypal deserted middle-aged wife has in mind
when she declares 'I gave him the best years of my life . . .'

Work and housework

Most women are housewives with prime responsibility for a
home and family. More than half of all married women also
work outside the home. A quick calculation therefore will
indicate that many women have two jobs, often both
demanding and full time. Feminists have focused increasingly
then on this dual nature of women's work, and investigated
the degree to which men's participation in housework has
risen along with women's participation in the labour force.
The findings in this area have not been very encouraging. In
1973 Young and Willmott in *The Symmetrical Family* failed
to find real symmetry in hours worked in the home. It was
evident even here that the *responsibility* for the home lay
entirely with the wife, and the husband was seen as a
subsidiary help with domestic chores. Moreover, if 'help' was
merely washing-up once a week, the husband was recorded
as contributing to housework. The pressure felt by working
wives was commented on by the authors. When asked if they
would prefer more pay or more time off, three-quarters of the
wives said they would choose more time at home. This was
not for leisure pursuits, however, but to be more effective
'looking after the family', 'giving more time to the children' or
'just catch[ing] up with the housework'. The men gave no

such response and were more likely to choose more pay than time off.[3] Although subsequently attacked for its male bias, *The Symmetrical Family* still indicated the very heavy workload of the working mother, the strain of two jobs, and constant over-tiredness: 'I have meals to get when I get home and there's the washing and ironing. There are always too many jobs. Then there's the tiredness. I get tired and get irritable with the children.'[4]

A more reliable guide to comparative time spent on household tasks is obtained by studies where men and women are asked to construct budgets of their time allocation. One such study in 1966 showed that employed women in both Britain and the USA spent almost twice as much time on household tasks as employed men. Women in the USA (a sample taken from 44 cities) spent 5¼ hours a day on household chores, in addition to their outside work.[5] A more recent study in Canada focused particularly on husbands and wives and showed that on an average weekend a woman would spend 33½ hours on housework, over against 8 hours spent by her husband. These latter hours would be largely in repairing and maintenance tasks and shopping. The same study showed that where there was no young child in the home, husbands increased their contribution to housework by only six minutes a week when their wives went out to work, bringing their contribution up to 3.3 hours a week![6]

A large number of studies come up with similar findings, by no means all of them conducted by feminist researchers. Nevertheless, they add to the feminists' case. The overall picture given is one of fatigue or even exhaustion suffered by many working wives who find it necessary to cut down on sleep, on leisure, on visiting and even on meals to keep their two roles together. Because many of them still feel 'guilty' about working outside the home, even though they know their earnings to be essential, there is often an anxiety that no one else in the household should suffer. A dirty shirt for the school concert can be all it takes to plunge some working mothers into despair and depression.

Housebound women
When the spotlight is on non-working wives and mothers what we are shown offers little more comfort. Housewives are by and large not happy about their situation. 70 per cent

of the women interviewed by Ann Oakley came out as 'dissatisfied' with housework: giving more complaints about monotony, fragmentation of work, and relentlessness of pace than factory workers in other studies. Although most women enjoyed the freedom of 'being their own boss' the pressure they felt under to 'keep up to standards' and maintain the routine meant that for many the freedom evaporated. Most women in her study resented the low status of their work: many felt a need to describe themselves in some other way because they felt that the social implications of being a housewife were those of being boring and uninteresting: 'When I think of a housewife it is of something not very nice to be—somebody who's got no interests outside the home.'[7]

Research done in both Britain and the USA has found in fact a high incidence of depression in married women who stay at home. An American study on psychological stress in adults maintained: 'Working women were overwhelmingly better off than the housewives. Far fewer than expected of the working women and more than expected of the housewives for example actually had a nervous breakdown . . .'[8] Of course, one can point out that this observation depends largely on what had been 'expected', and therefore is hardly hard data. Nevertheless incidence of nervousness, inertia, insomnia, shaking, nightmares, fainting, headaches, dizziness and heart palpitations were high on the list of symptoms experienced by housebound women. It is also true from other studies that monotony, depression, loneliness and boredom do feature in many accounts of housebound wives. 'You could be murdered here and no one would know. When the milkman comes it's an event.' 'You tend to get this feeling that unless you get out and talk to someone you'll go stark, raving mad.'[9]

Different ways out of the boredom are attempted: from escape into the interminable TV soap operas available every afternoon for American housewives, to obsessive shopping or bargain hunting, to over-involvement with housework. In each case an unreal world becomes the substitution for the dissatisfying real one. An imaginary life can be identified with, and drama played out daily on the screen. The characters are easy to relate to and undemanding: a world of glamour, interest and intrigue is available at the touch of a switch. The successful ratings of *Dallas* and *General Hospital* tell their own story. Alternatively, the idol of an ideal home can become the focus, where the same job is done over and over again each day to ensure perfection. Many women in Ann Oakley's study cleaned the house from top to bottom every day, washing the floors several times a day, and yet felt uneasy because there were still times when the house was not perfect. A 'perfect' home seemed to be one which betrayed no signs of any occupation. In a day of labour saving devices many women still spend up to 100 hours a week on house-related tasks.

Motherhood

The position of women as mothers has been the subject of critical analysis by many feminist writers since the late 1960s. Stereotypes of mothers as instinctively prepared and fulfilled in their reproductive role have been constantly challenged. The notion that motherhood is a totally pleasurable and satisfying experience, that it gives meaning and enrichment to a woman's life, has been countered by evidence showing that for many women motherhood is more a time of conflict, exhaustion, the sense of years slipping away, isolation and lack of personal identity. The conflict is between feelings of tenderness towards the children coupled with anger and resentment, and inability to cope. Many women who come to crisis centres fearing that they will damage their children, find their frustrations and anger uncontrollable, although few say they have no love for their children. Conflict arises too because the needs of the children are often manifestly different from the mother's own needs. The unpreparedness of new mothers for the constant and often insatiable demands of a totally dependent infant is also well documented. The fact that their performance is often being assessed by professional 'others', who frequently give conflicting advice, can also undermine their confidence.

A frequent complaint from feminists, then, is that the media presentation of motherhood, of gentle, patient women joyfully tending happy, bouncing babies is not matched in many mothers' real experiences. Nor does the picture necessarily improve as children grow older. A loss of identity outside motherhood is a common problem which stores up trouble when the children become independent. In many societies this identification of a woman with her wifely or motherly role is very pronounced. In America in particular women often come together as their children's mothers or their husbands' wives. (Staff wives, faculty wives, clergy wives, or 'school' mothers, 'team' mothers, 'nursery' mothers.) It is not unusual for women to be identified with their husband's position and department, or their children's class or grade. (Mrs John X, professor of biology, or Mrs Doe of grades four and five.) In other societies, of course, women do not even take their husbands' surname (in the Sudan, for example).

It is the way that the modern conception of motherhood has forced women into isolation, and played down their own needs and their own unique identities which has led many feminist writers to challenge the ethos behind it. High on the list of questions is whether being a mother need entail having (almost) sole responsibility for the care and nurture of children. Studies on maternal deprivation which claim to show alarming consequences of children being deprived of maternal care are repudiated as being methodologically unsound. Instead, communal care, wider familial care, a pattern of rotating responsibility for children are all proposed as perfectly viable alternatives. These all have the advantage of easing some of the burden from a mother's shoulders. Much more radical solutions are also posed, of course, and we shall be considering these more in the next section.

Violence in the home

Male violence against women has always been high in the concerns of the feminists, but it was not until the 1970s that the problem of physical abuse in the home was fully opened up. A small minority of women had always been known to suffer at the hands of their husbands but this had been seen as a freak phenomenon: the product of a disturbed personality or a bitterly unhappy marriage. The British Women's Aid campaign of the 1970s challenged all that, showing that the problem was widespread and that wives of the community's 'élite' were as likely to be beaten as wives of ex-convicts. They therefore reinterpreted the problem and its cause: 'Domestic violence was about power. It was not, any more than was rape, an explosion of testosterone, and although alcohol was often used as an excuse, wife battering was often planned . . . and in many ways amounted to quite systematic and deliberate torture.'[10] Women slashed by razors, women with broken ribs, disfigured faces, torn hair and skin, were all amongst those who sought help at the first Women's Aid refuge set up in Brixton in 1973. Two years later thirty similar refuges had opened in England. Similar centres were being established in other countries.

In 1974 a Select Committee was set up to review the problem of domestic violence, and the Domestic Violence Act became law in 1976. The Act made it legally possible for the violent spouse to be excluded from the joint home by injunction. Women now no longer had to initiate divorce proceedings before the injunction could be issued. However, until the Housing Act (Homeless Persons) followed in 1977, a physically abused woman was still left with problems. For many excluded violent spouses would return to the marital home to take their revenge, and many battered wives were afraid to continue to live there. The Housing Act declared the victim of violent abuse to be 'homeless', and local authorities now had the responsibility of providing housing in this situation.

Although legislation can never itself prevent people from damaging each other, it can *protect* the victim. However, by 1981 research groups were showing that the law had been comparatively ineffective in the protection it offered. Thousands of women had applied for injunctions, and the majority of those studied had been granted one; nevertheless the onus remained on the victim to prove that a man 'really was' violent. It seemed often that only badly bruised or beaten women, with visible scars, were able to offer this proof. Women reported too that the police had been reluctant to answer calls for help, even when they had an injunction. They were even more reluctant to press charges.

Breakdown and divorce
The feminists' final case against marriage as a woman's route to happiness rests with the divorce figures. Set against the growing unpopularity of marriage (14 per cent of all women now cohabit outside marriage) and the postponement of many weddings until the couple has lived together (20 per cent of single women live with their husbands before marriage) divorce statistics are even more striking. In 1961 32,000 divorce petitions were filed. By 1970 this had almost doubled

to 72,000. Ten years later in 1980 the figure stood at 170,000, bringing Britain almost into line with the high divorce rates associated with the United States. In America it is estimated that about half of all marriages end in divorce. In Britain the figure is between a half and a third. Divorce legislation can certainly account for some of the increase. The changes brought about by the 1971 law removed the need to prove matrimonial blame or guilt, and the concept of irretrievable breakdown without adultery having been committed became legally effective.

However, the feminist case is not merely that more people are divorcing. It is also that there is a crucial difference in the number of petitions filed by men and women. In 1961 husbands filed 14,000 petitions for divorce and wives filed 18,000. In 1971 these figures stood at 44,000 over 67,000. In 1981 husbands still filed 46,000 divorce petitions, but the figure filed by wives had risen to 123,000! Women, then, are seeking three-quarters of all the divorce petitions considered. Again the feminists would agree that there are a number of explanations for this. It could be that on the whole women find it easier to obtain satisfactory maintenance orders if they are the ones to ask for divorce. It may be, and often is, that the woman is the one deserted, and the one left with the job of formally ending the marriage. But it is also that women are less prepared to endure prolonged infidelity, neglect or an empty marriage than they were a generation ago. Because of a greater degree of financial independence many more women are no longer totally dependent on a husband's income.

At the same time as endorsing the need for a woman to be independent of an unhappy marriage, feminist writers nevertheless point out that in fact in many divorces women do suffer enormously. Usually they are the ones awarded custody of children, and their husbands are the ones who should continue to maintain the family financially. However, the difficulty experienced by mothers in obtaining payment after divorce is now well documented. It is suggested that not many more than one third of husbands are still maintaining their children a year after divorce, and fewer than twelve per cent continue to their children's adulthood. In the United States the situation is even worse, as there is very little post-divorce financial provision for wives. Women in late middle age are particularly vulnerable: the figures indicate they are far less likely to remarry, often have poor career prospects, and may have few friends of their own after being housewives for twenty-five years. In the United States womens' groups themselves have formed to offer support and training through very difficult post divorce situations.

In making the feminist case in the area of marriage and the family I am aware that many who are reading this will feel that the emphasis has been unreasonably negative. Many will find little to identify with in the descriptions they give of abuse, divorce, or even motherhood or housework. It will be encouraging if this is so. At the same time there will be those who are able to identify areas of their own lives in what they have read. That these problems are the experience of *many* women is nevertheless undeniable. What we need to ask all along is what is the real diagnosis, and what solutions can be offered.

Notes

1. Gerald Brenan writing of Dorothy Pritchard; quoted in M. Glastonbury, *Inspiration and Drudgery* (WRRC Publications 1978), p. 35.
2. Studies here include 'It's a Pleasure to Cook for Him' in Eva Gamarnikov (ed.) *et al.*, *Public and Private*, Heinemann 1983.
3. M. Young and P. Willmott, *Symmetrical Family: Study of Work and Leisure in the London Region.* Penguin 1975, p. 115, table 16.
4. ibid., p. 117.
5. Quoted from I. Cullen, 'A Day in the Life of . . .' (*New Society,* 28, 1974), pp. 63, 65.
6. Meissner and Humphreys, 'No Exit for Wives' (*Canadian review of Sociology and Anthropology,* 12 (4), 1975), pp. 424, 439.
7. Ann Oakley, *Housewife* (Penguin 1976), p. 100.
8. J. Bernard, *The Future of Marriage: His and Hers* (Souvenir Press 1975), p. 47.
9. *Housewife,* p. 101.
10. E. Wilson, *What is to be Done About Violence Against Women?* (Penguin 1983), p. 199.

3: Women in the Professions

The presence of women in the professions is often cited as evidence that sexism in society is not nearly so rampant as some would imagine. There are women doctors, solicitors, architects, educationalists, accountants, economists, engineers, hospital administrators, bankers, members of parliament, and even women prime ministers. Women make decisions which affect each one of us in our everyday lives. In some professions — medicine and teaching — women in fact dominate the field. It would seem clear then that any argument about sexual inequality in society would have to exclude the professions, where women of high ability and education work as equals alongside the most highly trained men, and earn the same salaries. What is more, this has been the case for a long time. It was as long ago as 1919 when the Sex Disqualification Removal Act was passed, creating a legal principle that neither sex nor marriage should disqualify a woman from carrying on any civil profession. Where a woman has the ability and determination she will get to the top. What holds women back is not any supposed discrimination but their own choice: many women choose to have children and be 'full-time' mothers, many others deliberately set their sights lower in order to combine domestic and work life.

So the image which is often created is that the professions are populated by highly intelligent, highly educated and highly motivated people of both sexes and that there are no bars to becoming a professional other than those of ability and choice. These commonly held assumptions are rejected by feminists who maintain that even a brief exploration of the situation which actually exists would produce an entirely different map.

History of women in the professions
One place to begin would be with a brief historical survey. In both Europe and the US some outstanding women had broken through into the professions in the mid-nineteenth century. Women medical students had been accepted in Zürich as

early as 1867. By 1879, after much opposition, the Massachusetts Medical Society opened its membership to women. In 1887 women were finally admitted to British Dental Schools, and in 1892, against further opposition, to the British Medical Association. The legal profession was equally hard for pioneering women to penetrate. Even in 1887 the Columbia College of Law in the US was refusing to admit women on the grounds that they 'had not the mentality to study law',[1] and it was not until the end of the century that a stronger foothold had been established. Women in accountancy had to wait much longer. Their proposed membership of the Society of Incorporated Accountants was soundly defeated in 1889.

However, the Act of 1919 certainly marked a watershed for women in the British professions, coming as it did on the heels of the enfranchisement of women over 30, and anticipating the 19th Amendment in the United States (1920). Quite quickly girls who had been held back from entering a number of professions at last found the legal bar removed. Even the ranks of the chartered accountants were penetrable. Now, articled women were able to take the final exam and qualify. Interestingly, the first to do so were daughters of leading chartered accountants. Similarly the Civil Service now became open to women, although it had its own restrictions by obliging its female employees to resign on marriage, a practice continued until 1946. In social work, too, women found a foothold. By 1921 some 60 per cent of social welfare related workers were women.

Yet a sober analysis of the changes brought by the 1919 Act will note that it did not open the floodgates to girls entering the professions. Daughters of professional men might well qualify, the Civil Service might well allow women to occupy its lower status jobs, some exceptional women might be called to the bar, or practise as doctors, but they were the exceptions which proved the rule. For in order to qualify one had to be trained, one had to have access to the universities, to medical and professional training schools, to the Inns of Court. Although British Universities could from 1875 confer degrees upon women if they wished, if they did not wish little could be done about it. Oxford and Cambridge did not wish, in spite of the presence of women's colleges and women students within the university. Oxford ended its 45 year denial to women in 1920, but it was not until 1947 that Cambridge's resistance to graduating its women finally gave way. In a similar vein, although women could and did enter the medical profession, there were no women at all in the London Medical Schools until 1948 when the University Grants commission insisted on a quota of 15 per cent.

This disparity between the legal openness of the professions and the difficulties experienced by women in moving into them did not end in the 1940s. The argument is that the professions even in the 1980s still exhibit a distinct male bias, and that when women enter the professions there is still the inbuilt expectation that they will occupy 'supportive' roles to their male counterparts. In fact, despite the assumptions of equality, professional jobs are still split along traditional gender lines: women are nurses, men are doctors; women are teachers, men are headmasters; women are social workers, men are social work directors; women are librarians, men are chief librarians; women are in the humanities, men are scientists and technologists; women are civil servants, men are permanent under-secretaries; women are deaconesses, men are bishops. The argument remains in fact that despite all appearances to the contrary the male domination of the professions has never been seriously challenged and that women today are not much more likely than they were in 1919 to reach the top echelons of their chosen career. To test this argument we need to focus on the contemporary scene.

The situation today: the male professions
In the majority of professions men outnumber women substantially at all levels. Figures from the late seventies showed that in the UK women formed 27 per cent of practising doctors, 23 per cent of journalists, 11 per cent of university teachers, 8 per cent of barristers, 5 per cent of architects, 4 per cent of solicitors, 2 per cent of engineers, 1 per cent of the Institute of Directors and 1 per cent of scientists and technicians.[2] They were similarly under-represented in accountancy, dentistry and in leading jobs in banking, insurance and the civil service. In the US the ratio was even lower in many professions. Even in 1982, of all registered physicians and dentists and other medical practitioners, only 14.6 per cent were women.[3]

Yet even these figures do not give an accurate picture. If we take university teaching alone, although 11 per cent of the total staff in Britain were women, only 6½ per cent of positions above lecturer were held by women, and fewer than 2 per cent of professorships. The situation is similar in medicine. Although more than a quarter of all doctors are women, about 87 per cent of all consultants are men. Yet even this can be misleading. For a glimpse at the top 'status' jobs in medicine—brain and heart surgery, chest and lungs, general surgery, neurology, bone surgery etc.—will reveal that almost all the consultancies are held by men. This is in fact echoed through a very long list. Where women do find a footing is in child psychiatry, family planning, obstetrics, and sometimes in pediatrics and gynaecology, although even here the *majority* of consultancies are held by men. Even in medicine then, the association of women doctors with women's and children's ailments is very evident. Many of the most prestigious areas of medicine have no women consultants at all.

We could take almost any of the other professions and find a similar pattern: a low ratio of women to men, with women almost totally unrepresented in the highest status and best paid jobs in the profession. Some would argue of course that to accept the common evaluation of worth in terms of status would be to move into a view of work which itself distorts its true value. This point is in fact important, and yet it only adds to what is wrong with the situation in the professions. That we have a distorted view of work and worth is often evident, but it does not eliminate the point that even *within* the distorted view, the view of women's work can be still more distorted.

Women's professions

We have focused on the majority of the professions so far, but there are three professions which exhibit a very different pattern. In nursing, librarianship and teaching women in fact form the majority of entrants into the profession. To a lesser extent it is also true of social work. The differences between these jobs and the others examined is strikingly obvious. The professional status is lower, salaries are lower, and the association of the jobs with traditional women's roles of child care and service to the weak and sick are obvious. By examining the teaching and librarianship professions the feminists' case is certainly strengthened.

It is claimed that in the teaching profession women come closer to equality with men than in most other forms of work. Teaching, too, has few of the problems for women associated with other jobs. For married mothers the school holidays are no problem, because they too are home with their children. There is rarely any weekend work, minimal overtime compared with some other jobs, and preparation work can all be done in the home. Teachers and children frequently arrive home at roughly the same time in the evening, so the problem over 'latch-key' children is rare. It is for these reasons that teaching has continued as a predominantly female profession. In fact around 59—60 per cent of all primary and secondary teachers in England and Wales are women.

However, it is with regard to the *distribution* of women within the teaching profession that the feminist case is made. In both Britain and the US women who teach subjects are far more likely to be found in the humanities, languages and domestic subjects than in science, economics or technology. But further, they are also far more likely to be found occupying the lowest scale positions than their male colleagues. For although in the UK, for example, men form only 41 per cent of the teaching profession, they occupy 62 per cent of all the headships. Focusing on elementary education alone, 78 per cent of all teachers in primary schools are women, yet they hold only 43 per cent of the headships.[4] Even in this profession then which women have made their own, and where women's expertise and skill at handling small children has been long acknowledged, the 22 per cent of male teachers run away with 57 per cent of the senior posts! This is echoed of course throughout teaching. Men are more likely than women to be heads of department and heads of year; men are more likely to teach at Grades 12 and 13 or sixth form level. Interestingly, in nursing, where few men have formerly been recruited, one finds male nurses increasingly at higher level posts.

One other profession needs to be mentioned. In librarianship we have probably the greatest anomaly of all. It is estimated that 80 per cent or more of all new entrants at degree or similar level are women, although a significant proportion do not stay on in the profession. Taking current figures overall, 60 per cent of those employed are women. Yet of the 108 top Grade 1 posts in English public libraries, 106 are filled by men: 98 per cent. Unlike the teaching profession where many women occupy deputy head positions, the second grade posts in librarianship are also overwhelmingly filled by men: 85 per cent of them. Similarly, the levels of salary throughout the profession are uneven. Most women librarians are on AP3, whereas the average pay level for most male librarians is AP5 — substantially higher. To the argument that the majority of women leave the profession before promotion is likely to occur, and thus distort the figures, it can be added that more than half the men who qualify also leave librarianship over the same period. In fact, the inequalities seem so pronounced that one woman researcher has argued that the odds against a woman reaching a Grade 1 administrative post in librarianship are 2,000 to 1![5]

Unambitious women?
If this sorely challenges the idea that the professions at least bring equality to women, is there any justification for the situation which exists? Could there be truth in the suggestion, for example, that women simply lack the ambition which drives people to the top: that women are not prepared to make the sacrifices for their careers which men are prepared to make?

There are two questions here. One concerns the alleged comparative 'ambitiousness' of men and women. Studies done suggest that to assume a lack of ambition on the part of the female sex in general as an explanation of the inequalities of promotion would be simply to create a scapegoat. This is not, for example, the conclusion of *Women in Top Jobs,* which looks at the progress of women in industrial management, the Civil Service, the BBC and architecture, and incidentally concludes that the last ten years has achieved very little for women's equality.[6] Nevertheless, it may well be true that in some professions women are ambitious for different things from those which lead to the top level administrative posts. In librarianship for instance, it is suggested that what attracts many women to the profession is contact with the public: the role of advising, selecting books, helping with research, and a hundred other tasks which involve face to face contact. Many women librarians questioned indicated that the facets of the highly paid administrative jobs which attracted them least were the distance from the reading public. In fact those jobs incorporated precisely that which women librarians found personally unrewarding and low in job satisfaction. Similar claims are often made for women in a whole range of professional and executive jobs.

This can hardly account for posts in medicine, however, where the highly regarded surgeons' jobs are those of the practitioners, not the administrators. Moreover, it would not explain why women do reach and seem content in highly administrative nursing posts, if nursing contact with the public is that which they value most.

The other suggestion was that women are not prepared to make the sacrifices for their careers which men are prepared to make. The first response again is that 'women' is too big a category to deal with in this way; some women are prepared to make sacrifices, some aren't. But another response challenges the assumptions behind the idea of professional 'sacrifice'. In fact the 'sacrifice' made by many professional men in the route to the top has been shown to be not so much a foregoing of their own personal pleasures (ambition for some is very pleasurable) but often a foregoing of family relationships. In very many cases indeed, it is a wife who makes the 'sacrifices' for her professional husband: sacrifices in terms of enjoying his company, in terms of her own career, in terms of deciding where they should live, in terms of conforming to the image expected of a director's wife, or a principal's wife, or a doctor's wife.[7] Such sacrifices which women make on a husband's behalf are not so readily expected of a husband on his wife's behalf. It would not be expected of a man that he gives up his career and becomes a full-time homemaker so that his professional and ambitious wife might 'get ahead'. So the 'sacrifices' of a professional man and a professional woman are not in the same category. It is seen as a struggle and a tension for a woman to combine both motherhood and demanding professional commitment, but until recently it has not been seen as a struggle for a man to combine both fatherhood and a career. Many young women applying for jobs are still asked if it is really worth appointing them when they might end up staying at home with children. It is extremely rare for a man to be asked this.

The isolated woman

There is one other aspect to the role of the professional woman in a 'man's world'. Frequently she will find herself very isolated. Much of the 'male talk' which goes on in non-work hours will not include her. Whilst she might fit in well professionally with her colleagues, 'after hours' she may well be the one who is not invited to their functions, their social gatherings or their husbands and wives parties — particularly if she is single. She may not be around on the golf course or in the club room where potential promotions are discussed. Often, in some very male dominant professions, she will find herself conforming to male expectations and male ethos, winning male approval in order to survive. This is why we find many professional women who have been 'firsts' in their field take an antagonistic stand against feminism. They have identified with 'male values' to such an extent that they see the question of promotion and professional development as one about agency and personal initiative, rather than about structural inequalities, where a few women leap the male-shaped hurdles, but the majority stay on the starting-line. It is to these structural explanations that we will turn in part two of the book.

Notes

1. Lois W. Banner, *Women in Modern America. A Brief History* (Harcourt Brace Jovanavich 1974), p. 35.
2. Lindsay Mackie and Polly Pattullo, *Women at Work* (Tavistock Publications 1977), pp. 73—4.
3. Figures supplied by the American Embassy, London 1984.
4. *D. E. S. Statistics of Education*, vol. 4, Teachers, 1978, table 12.
5. Sheila Ritchie, '2000 to 1: Sex Oddity' (*Assistant Librarian* March 1979), pp. 38—41. See also S. Jespersen, 'The Problems Faced by Women in Libraries' (*Librarians for Social Change* vol. 4 no. 1), pp. 3—5.
6. Michael Fogarty, Isobel Allen and Patricia Walters, Policy Studies Institute, *Women in Top Jobs 1968—1979* (Heinemann Educational Books 1981), pp. 117, 119.
7. Janet Finch, *Married to the Job*. George Allen and Unwin 1983.

4: Education for Girls

Dr Johnson said, 'A man is better pleased when he has a good dinner on the table than when his wife talks Greek.'[1] Nor was he alone in his sentiments. But two hundred years later in the Crowther Report 1959 education for girls was envisaged as teaching them how to cook a good dinner for the table *and* how to talk Greek. The 'dual role' of women of home and career became institutionalized into educational theory. The 1963 Robbins Report echoed a similar theme, talking of the untapped pools of ability which would become tappable with the expansion of the universities. Yet the dual role was seen really for middle-class girls. For girls from the working classes the educational emphasis remained largely on preparing for the single role of housework and childrearing. The result was, of course, that a large proportion of these girls went into jobs which required no training.

Although there was a sudden interest in teaching girls science around this period no one was under any illusion about their basic ineptitude for these subjects. Newsom reported in 1963:

A boy is usually excited by the prospect of a science course . . . he experiences a sense of wonder and power. The growth of wheat, the birth of a lamb, the movement of clouds, put him in awe of nature; the locomotive he sees as man's response; the switch and throttle are his magic wands . . . The girl may come to the science lesson with a less eager curiosity than the boy but she too will need to feel at home with machinery.[2]

A large number of assumptions was built into the way in which educating boys and girls was seen even at this period of expansion. There was no suggestion of educating men for dual roles of fatherhood and work. Nor was a very satisfactory attempt made to equip the women singled out for this attention. Most girls had to choose beween domestic and academic subjects very early, and 'intelligent' girls were the ones who chose academic subjects. The problem over reconciling the two roles must be faced later. One way out would always be to employ a woman without the same educational level, who could relieve her of the less well-paid tasks.

Another concern came into view during this time. Westergaard and Little, writing in 1965, emphasized the fundamental handicap of the working-class child, particularly if that child were female. There was disparity between the sexes all the way along the line, but it became acute further down the social scale: 'At the extreme of the scale, the unskilled manual worker's daughter has a chance of only one in five or six hundred of entering a university—a chance a hundred times lower than if she had been born into a professional family.'[3] Six years later Ronald King reported that even within the state system a working-class girl had twenty-one times less chance of taking a university degree than a middle-class boy.[4]

Since then of course there has been considerable movement in the curriculum. Boys have been encouraged to take cooking and domestic subjects, although these are frequently dropped by the third year. Girls are more likely to be found in science classes than they were, although they are still more likely to be studying biology rather than physics or chemistry. Yet although there have been some shifts, the redistribution of students at undergraduate level remains along the old gender lines. More boys than girls will be studying degree courses to start with. They will outnumber women in every area except languages, education and the arts. University statistics published in 1982 showed that in some fields the gap remained enormous. 34,200 men studied engineering and technology but only 2,500 women. More than twice as many men than women studied science, architecture and agriculture. It seems that, despite much weaning away at a public level, attitudes to education still indicate rigid gender divisions.[5]

Is science masculine?
Investigating the low response of girls to science as a career has brought interesting results. It has not indicated that girls are mentally less capable of coping with abstractions or experimental details. But there has been a suggestion that the masculine image given to science often prevents girls from taking it up. Three important points have been put forward. First, a widespread lack of confidence amongst girls has put them off tackling science subjects which are often presented as difficult. Even though those girls who do go on to study

sciences at 'O' level do not find them significantly more difficult than other subjects this 'difficult' image has already deterred many others. Second, the close identification of science with men means that it is unattractive to girls who are at a stage of forming their own sexual identity. Anything 'unfeminine' may be threatening, and may mark a girl out. The much higher take-up of science subjects in all-girls schools suggests that where the masculine associations are absent the subjects are more attractive. Careers advice too often reinforces these images, and steers girls away from technology or engineering, stressing the difficulties they may have to encounter. Third, science may be taught and presented in a very impersonal, detached manner, in a way that does not appeal to girls socialized into a caring role. It will be interesting to see if the various projects designed to counteract some of these issues will come up with new ways of teaching and presenting science in a way which can benefit not only girls but boys too.

Roles at school

The issues raised in a discussion of girls and science have much deeper implications and concern education for girls as a whole. For the conclusions arrived at are that it is not anything in the biological or brain composition of girls which makes them either under-achievers, or prone to certain subjects. It is rather the climate in which they are growing up and being taught. Schools are notorious for enforcing gender roles on children, not through teachers only, but through peer interaction. From the earliest stage certain behaviour is deemed appropriate for the different sexes. At playschool boys will not be discouraged from climbing, banging cars, and noisy playground games, although girls will not be expected to perform in this way. Girls will more likely be left in groups of one or two to play dolls or houses. It is assumed that because it occurs at this age this behaviour is somehow 'natural', but in fact it is that which is reinforced by parents and teachers. Little boys are encouraged to be adventurous, expected to be rougher, untidier and less well-mannered than girls. Sex differences are frequently exaggerated in the classroom:

Phrases such as 'two strong boys to carry the desk', 'a responsible girl to sit with the infants', 'sit quietly like the girls', 'he's a cissy', 'she's a tomboy' are common. It has been estimated that at school pupils are classified by sex approximately 40 times a day. Thus children learn the stereotypes of girl and boy and how they are supposed to behave.[6]

This will of course have repercussions on both what they choose to study later and how well they do academically. But it will stretch further than that. It will provide as strong a curriculum as anything formally on the timetable. Through these kinds of reinforced suggestions, far more than through working with text books comes a child's ideas of what everyday life is about, and of her place in it. If it is continually indicated to her that good girls are passive and co-operative, then she will either internalize the image and model herself on it in order to gain approval, or she will rebel and see herself as deviant. This will not be deviant for the boy, however. Although irritating, his independence is seen as masculine and appropriate for his future role in society, and it will be reinforced in many different ways in the school. In *Invisible Woman* Dale Spender argues that both staff and pupils bring an assumption of male precedence into the classroom, with the result that boys are given a disproportionate amount of attention.[7]

Feminists argue then that it is not simply a matter of what is taught to whom. School is the place where basic attitudes, gender roles, and acceptable behaviour are all communicated. It is the place where even the most non-sexist start in the early home life can be jeopardized. It is the place where authority is seen residing in male hands, where science and technology are seen as male subjects taught mostly by male teachers, where story time and textbooks and TV aids are usually about boys and men, and where a manifestly different attitude is demonstrated to girls' and boys' behaviour. Often a gender war is initiated in the classroom: girls' teams against boys' teams. I have been in one classroom where a form of punishment for a boy was to sit with the girls. Deeply engrained attitudes about the place of men and women in society, and unresolved basic questions about how to, or whether to, educate girls for two roles surface continually in our educational programmes and make schools a place of learning, but also of some confusion for many girls.

Notes

1. Quoted in Lindsay Mackie and Polly Pattullo, *Women at Work* (Tavistock Publications 1977), p. 26.
2. *Newsom Report* (HMSO 1963), p. 142.
3. Westergaard and Little, *Educational Opportunity and Social Selection in England and Wales* (Paris OECD 1965), p. 222; quoted in Byrne *Women and Education* (Tavistock Publications 1978), p. 249.
4. Quoted in Course Unit of U221, *The Changing Experience of Women*, Unit 13 (Open University Press 1983), p. 18.
5. Alison Kelly, 'Why Girls Don't Do Science' (*New Scientist* 20 May 1982), p. 499.
6. *Equal Opportunities Commission, Seventh Annual Report* (HMSO 1982), p. 71.
7. Dale Spender, *Invisible Women: The Schooling Scandal.* Writers and Readers 1982.

5: Women and the Law

This century has been described as the 'woman's epoch' because of the number of legal reforms which have favoured women. In fact the process started earlier: legislation from the late nineteenth century onwards has greatly affected women's economic, social and political situation. Gradually, married women have been given property rights, equality in the grounds for divorce, legal aid, custody of children, child benefit, and maintenance after divorce. Women in general have received the vote, the right to a university education, entry into the professions, and access to a wide range of jobs. Especially since the 1960s, with so many laws passed prohibiting discriminatory advertising, enforcing equal pay, changing matrimonial law, enforcing maintenance provisions, establishing the right to the marital home, and with abortion law reform, it is argued that women have had more than their fair share of attention from the legislators. What is more, women now have it both ways. Whilst being allowed equal pay for equal work in Britain they nevertheless retire at sixty with full pension, whilst men struggle on for five more years. Again, even though divorced men can claim maintenance from their wives, in the vast majority of cases the law still gives divorced women a 'meal ticket for life'. What is more, in a dispute over children after divorce the courts are still much more likely to award custody to the mother and leave the father with a constant fight for access. It is the mother too, who, with the consent of two doctors, makes the final decision about an abortion. When a father opposed his wife's decision in the courts his case was dismissed. A woman can get her husband turned out of his own house if he beats or mistreats her, whereas it would be extremely difficult for a man to obtain the same legal enforcement. In fact, it looks like a win hands down for the feminists: women have the law quite unfairly on their side.

Some of the legal issues we have mentioned are very complex, and all this brief chapter can do is to reflect on whether or not this area does demonstrate a massive feminist breakthrough. The feminists themselves think not. It is interesting too that this is the conclusion of both British and

American feminists, even though the legal systems of those countries are markedly different. In attempting to compare and assess their cases it will be necessary to ask much deeper questions about the nature of law, and its relationship to other areas of life.

Law in Britain

I want to focus on the arguments of the British feminists first. Their initial point is that all the legislation passed needs to be put in the perspective of where women started from. Legally, women started from nothing. They had no part in the political process, and the few economic and legal rights which they did possess disappeared on marriage. The principle of 'femme couverte' dominated British law. Blackstone's famous *Commentaries* summarized the situation: 'By marriage the husband and wife are one person in law; that is, the very being or legal existence of the woman is suspended during the marriage, or at least incorporated and consolidated into that of the husband.'[1]

A woman then legally ceased to exist on marriage. She could not own property, incur debts, enter any contract or sue for loss. Her husband had sole jurisdiction over their children and could appoint a guardian over them after his death against any wishes of his wife. These legal deprivations were not seen however as punitive: 'Even the difficulties which the wife lies under are for the most part intended for her protection and benefit,'[2] an issue we will be examining later.

That understanding of law persisted well into the nineteenth century, so legislation from the mid-century onwards has merely been chipping away at the massive legal bias towards men. What looks like a lot of reforms is only an attempt to redress a very unequal balance. Many would have us believe, however, that it has been an overwhelming success. As long ago as 1930 Judge McCardie claimed: 'I find privileges given to a wife which are wholly denied to a husband, and I find that upon the husband has fallen one "injustice upon another".'[3] It is interesting, of course, that although *he* found them the vast majority of women found otherwise. What is more, matrimonial law, legal aid, custody of children and maintenance, provisions all created since the learned judge gave his dictum have still not been able to ameliorate the economic dependence and hardship which many divorced wives encounter. In areas other than family law the position is no better. Laws couched in terms of equality within inequal structures end up often by creating more discrimination. We have seen already how an Equal Pay Act is ineffective or even counter-productive when women do not have real access to the same jobs as men. This was one of the reasons why many earlier reformers concentrated on *protective* legislation for women: a form of legislation still working on the concepts outlined by Blackstone above.

Common law and the judiciary

A deeper reason why parliamentary laws have not brought equality lies in the nature of the British legal system itself. For, unlike the US, law in Britain is not embodied in a constitution and its amendments, and added to by state and federal laws. A very large proportion of British law is 'common law'. The judiciary in fact creates its own legal precedents, and these are then incorporated into the whole legal framework. Much law education involves the learning of volumes of case studies and being able to apply the judgements and rulings in those to a new case which now emerges. There are, of course, appeals against judgements: both in terms of using inappropriate precedents, or not satisfactorily weighing the current evidence. But in the end the appeals themselves are heard by judges and everything stays of course within the judicial sphere, never returning to that other law-maker, parliament. So the parliamentary process in law-making is in many ways only marginal. A great deal is left to the judiciary.

It is when we look more closely at the judiciary that another of the feminist arguments comes to the fore. Judges are very largely male. They are often elderly, and conservative in their views of sex roles and relationships between men and women. This need not of course lead to any deliberate attempt to give unfair judgements. Impartiality before the law is a principle which most British judges would be very concerned to uphold and maintain. Nevertheless, judges themselves do reflect attitudes and stereotypes about women held in society at large. Because much legislation is inevitably 'flabby' and needs to be interpreted in each different situation 'rights' can easily become confused with conventions, or with what *seems* right from the judge's (male) point of view.

Expectations about 'normal' male and female behaviour can of course come into play in many judgements. In rape cases, judgement has more than once been made for a defendant on the grounds that the protesting and struggling woman had by her appearance, location, manners or dress, somehow 'asked for it'. No judge can be uninfluenced by his own attitudes and ideas. Even the gracious and very gentle Lord Denning, a good friend to women, had nevertheless very fixed ideas about what was right and proper for a woman. There is much evidence that before the 1970s reforms he saw her 'legal' rights as bound up with her moral integrity.

So the idea of the courts as there to uphold the neutral and objective rules of the land, as decided by parliament, is a naive one. The reality is that judges make decisions according to precedents set by former judges and reflecting their own ideas of justice, propriety and what is 'normal'. These ideas themselves of course embody attitudes, stereotypes and prejudices which are in many senses culture-bound and gender-bound, and therefore by no means neutral.

Legal agents
The next point takes the gender issue further, and is an argument which American feminists would also echo. It is that in addition to the judiciary, most of the others involved in the law are also male. Out of 650 Members of Parliament only twenty-three are women. Similarly in Congress only twenty-two out of 435 members of the House of Representatives are women and only two out of 100 in the Senate.[4] Solicitors and barristers are predominantly male, and so is the police force. Because they are all likely to have similar views about women, the women involved will often feel 'up against it' on all accounts. It is in fact often very difficult for a policeman, a lawyer, a judge or a parliamentarian to see a situation from a woman's point of view. Because to be male is to be normal, it makes sense that the law itself, and the application of the law, should reflect this normality. It is easy to make allowances for male behaviour, because even if it is unwise or even illegal it is understandable. As men ourselves, we know the pressures that other men might have to face. On the other hand, female behaviour is something quite different:

often irrational, unreasonable, frequently ungrateful. Even when because of the concerted efforts of women's pressure groups, aided by reformist men, the law is changed, the attitudes of law-enforcers can make even the most carefully worded piece of legislation ineffective.

This is one of the reasons why the majority of rape cases never reach the courts. Attitudes of the police to victims of alleged rape are now well illustrated, and one example was shown a few years ago on a TV documentary for all to see. Even though in many places in Britain and the US rape complaints and allegations are now handled by women officers, the overriding lack of sympathy from the majority of male policemen deters all but the most determined from pursuing their case. Even then they have to be prepared for the defence lawyer to rake up any irrelevant mud in order to produce the desired image of the 'rape' victim as a probably promiscuous woman, and the 'rape', by implication, as intercourse with consent. Some women who have unsuccessfully brought rape cases to court have argued that only if they had been scarred, slashed or damaged for life would the court have accepted that there had really been a struggle. Women who protect themselves from the rapist by not resisting to the point of violence or physical danger often find themselves with no case to bring. The police show a similar suspicion of or disinterest in the woman's story in cases of domestic violence. Again, although legally empowered to intercede in the home they show themselves very reluctant to exercise this prerogative. Nor do they show great vigilance in confiscating obscene literature and publications, even when there is quite open defiance of the pornography laws. Indeed when action along these lines is taken, it usually causes quite a sensation. One reason for this will now be evident. No matter how much it debases and dehumanizes women, an interest in pornography is seen as somehow 'natural' for a man.

Power relations

This legal process is often presented as being about the just application of law in a largely consensus society. Most of us know what is just, and most of us agree that the law should be upheld. This is again naive on two accounts. The idea of consensus in our society, although appealed to by the legislators and by governments, is an over-optimistic one.

Governments are not on the whole given the massive 'mandate from the people' which the Thatcher and Reagan administrations both claimed. In Britain at least they are voted in using an archaic electoral system which ensures that a quarter of the electorate or more will be unrepresented. Similarly many of their laws are not 'endorsed by the people'; they are at best merely tolerated.

However, the second point is more pertinent to our discussion here. It is that rather than being the objective application of a law which everyone accepts, the legal process is much more about bargaining and power relationships. Here law provides the framework for bargaining and many feminists argue that what women need is to be able to improve their bargaining position. However, since that position itself depends on other factors—knowledge of the law, ability to buy advice, and the economics to pursue their case—women here are generally in a weaker situation than those with whom they are bargaining. The courts themselves play relatively little part in this. In fact the vast majority of civil litigation is settled out of court, and this is especially important in the area of matrimonial law.

The argument that the law is about power relationships is presented in other ways. The 'professionalization' of the legal process puts the layman at the mercy of lawyers whose expertise they are forced to accept. What is more there is little redress if negligence on the part of the lawyer occurs or is suspected. Although there are legal aid provisions in certain circumstances, the hiring of lawyers is otherwise a very costly business and the work undertaken can be minimal. (In the US of course lawyers can advertise for clients, and in particular competitive rates for non-contested divorce business appear in every newspaper.) Again, since most lawyers are men, and not well-known for their pastoral skills, some women with few financial resources and unsure of their legal rights feel intimidated before the whole process begins. They experience their own lack of power in an acute and often overwhelming way.

In some areas of course a woman might have some help with the bargaining process. In cases of unequal pay or unfair dismissal she may well persuade the relevant union to take up her case. This may not of course be easy, not only because she may not be a union member herself, but because the interests of the male majority might be in conflict with hers. However, women are often involved in litigation where unions would be of no help. It is to the area of matrimonial law, particularly as it exists in Britain today, that we now briefly turn.

Matrimonial law

Because the assumptions behind 'femme couverte' have endured longer than the legal principle, the marital area has been one of the most hotly debated legal areas. Even after the nineteenth-century reforms it was still not until 1923 that the law gave women equal grounds for divorce. It is the most recent Matrimonial Causes Act, however, which sets the context for the debate today. Since 1971 the basis of the divorce law has been changed from that of marital blame to that of 'irretrievable breakdown' (or 'no fault' divorce as it is known in the US). Instead of having to prove adultery, desertion or neglect on the part of the guilty spouse, a divorce can be obtained after two years' separation by a couple simply agreeing that their marriage has irretrievably broken down. The contrast with the previous law comes most strongly in the next clause because, as long as a couple have lived apart for five years, a divorce can be obtained against the wishes of one partner. Concretely, this means that in the archetypal case a middle-aged successful man might abandon a faithful stay-at-home wife for a new partner, whom he is free to marry after five years. He can then confer on her the financial provisions and long-term benefits which his wife might have helped to produce and might have expected to enjoy. Clearly then, for cases like this, as well as for more complex others, careful consideration has to be given to issues of custody of children and maintenance after divorce.

These are in fact areas of much current feminist interest for, even though the law provides general guidelines, the position is very much one of bargaining. The guidelines themselves take several possible forms. The ⅓—⅓ principle, established by Lord Denning, argues that divorced women should be eligible to one third of the current property and other assets, and one third of the income. Other interpretations of the legal provisions are built on the 'clean break' principle: that rather than leaving the wife dependent on a continual and perpetual 'hand-out' from a possibly unco-operative husband, the provision should be made now once and for all. So the outright transfer of capital assets, such as the marital home, is one way of deciding this. Again one can see the considerable problems, where a husband may have limited capital assets now, but his future circumstances might be much more favourable. Thus, deciding the matter in the light of present financial circumstances might well be strongly against the interests of the wife. Often the bargaining focuses upon the marital home. Legally, the wife now has the right to stay in the family home until the children are old enough to leave. Often the courts fix a period after which the house must be sold and the money divided, even though the house may technically be in the husband's name. The wife will often then be left to her own resources, which might not of course amount to much.

In many cases then, although the law has made it possible for a fairer treatment for wives, because of the bargaining situation many wives do settle for less than they might be entitled to if they pushed the matter through. In many cases women have no position of strength to bargain from. In the case mentioned earlier, because of the wife's dependence on her husband's salary, and because she has been indirectly contributing to the development of his career rather than her own she is indeed extremely vulnerable if the marriage ends in divorce. With few skills to get a well-paid job, lack of confidence in her ability and her personal worth, and now on her own, the future can look unpromising. In some such cases of course the deserting spouse's sense of justice, and his long-term concern, will override his desire to wrench what he can from his former wife. But it is a sad fact that in the majority of cases the concern and consideration is transferred quite abruptly to the new partner, and of course to the husband's own self-interest. The suggestion of maintaining the standard of living for a discarded wife has received much vocal resistance from the Campaign for Justice in Divorce—a male backlash against maintenance provision.

Protective legislation
On the face of it protective legislation is bound to reinforce inequality. The very assumptions behind it are that women are not to be seen on the same legal footing as men: they are

in need of protection. The law then is to prevent the exploitation of women as the weaker and more vulnerable sex. In particular cases it serves to ensure that women need not work the same number of hours as men, or be available for the same shift or overtime work. Most of the factory acts of the nineteenth century stemmed from these provisions. Similarly today, we see the same assumptions behind maintenance provision, the earlier retirement age, the exclusion of women from work in coal mines, and a number of other legal features.

Feminists are usually in two minds about this whole argument. On the one hand, equality in work and in marital and economic relations will never come if women are seen differently in this fundamental legal way. So one body of feminist thinking argues that we should move away from this concept of law altogether. At the same time, however, another group maintains that if protective legislation were to be removed then exploitation would certainly occur. If women were *required* to do the same shifts and overtime as men then certainly wage rates would be closer. However, given the present social situation it is clear that children would suffer, members of the family would rarely be all together, and the additional burden of organizing and caring for a very complicated family life would fall on women. This fear, of course, is what makes those who argue for the removal of protective legislation also argue very vehemently for 24-hour nurseries.

The Equal Rights Amendment

A discussion of woman and law cannot be concluded without a brief look at the American Equal Rights Amendment. The legal structure which operates in the United States is much more centred around the written Constitution than that in Britain. Different states may have their separate laws but these are seen as further upholding the constitutional framework. That is why in order to gain real equality for women American feminists see the necessity of amending the Constitution. The Equal Rights Amendment was the proposal, and introduced into Congress each year since 1923. However, it has had a chequered history, coming up against the 'New Right' in the 1980s whose opposition proved too strong. It had passed both the House of Representatives and the Senate in 1972, and by 1978 thirty-four state legislatures had ratified the amendment. Since it was so close to the required ratification of three-quarters of the states the period was extended until 1982. However, the Republican party removed the ERA from its platform in 1980, and four months later the incoming President was known for his opposition to the proposed amendment. Its defeat in 1982 was without much surprise. Its future under a new administration remains to be seen.

What the amendment says is simple enough. It is that equality of rights under the law shall not be denied or abridged by the United States or by any state on account of sex, and gives Congress power to enforce this by appropriate legislation. Since this is so evidently in keeping with the rest of the American Constitution, opposition to this twenty-seventh amendment needs to be given some attention.

Although opposition is most easily identified with the New Right, the opponents come from many viewpoints. There are those who, as in our previous section, suggest that the inevitable abolition of all protective legislation would be harmful. Far from removing discrimination it would initially make women more vulnerable. Since the effects of any ERA would take many years, or decades, women in the meantime would be returned to the inequalities before protective legislation. Then there are those who argue against the amendment with regard to specific aspects: some are unhappy that it would mean women would have to be included in any future military service conscription. Others see in it an implicit acceptance of abortion, others are unhappy about the implications for alimony and the undermining of the traditional view of marriage. Finally, there are those who oppose it on constitutional grounds. Whilst often supporting equal rights in principle they argue that a constitutional amendment is not necessary to ensure this. Both the fifth and the fourteenth amendments cover the proposals of the ERA. Constitutionally, women already have equality. Needless to say this is rejected by its supporters on the grounds that neither the fifth nor fourteenth amendments had women in mind: that the nineteenth amendment concerned only the vote, and that once an amendment spelled out the equality of women, it would be incontrovertible.

However, even the most loyal supporters of the ERA do not

expect that the amendment itself will bring instant change. As in Britain, the law and the constitution provide only the legal framework in which we live. Attitudes and stereotypes will need greater transformation than that afforded by the law alone.

Notes

1. Blackstone's *Commentaries* vol. 1, bk 1 (London, A. Strachan, Law Printer, 1809), chap. 15, sect. 111, p. 441.
2. ibid., p. 445 (see note 23).
3. Judge McCardie: Gottliffe v. Edelston 1930; quoted in 'The Position of Women in Family Law', Julia Brophy and Carol Smart, in E. Whitelegg (ed.) *et al., The Changing Experience of Women* (Martin Robertson, Oxford 1982), p. 211.
4. As from UK elections June 1983 and USA Presidential election 19 November 1984.

6: Women and the Church

Most feminists do not mount any detailed criticism of sexual inequality within the Church. For them the Church itself signifies oppression. The Church is beyond redemption. It is that institution which has in the past contributed most soundly to subduing women, and has provided a divine justification for doing so: 'Male religious authority reinforces male secular authority, and gives it a mystical unquestionable basis.'[1] Yet now the Church is archaic, out of touch and largely irrelevant. In 600 pages of *The Female World* Jessie Bernard commits less than two pages to 'Religion and the Church'.[2] Women who still see some meaning and significance in Christian commitment and church worship are on the whole to be pitied. For whilst they willingly accept the whole male-centred ideology, the deification of manhood along with the crippling moral taboos it places on women, then their liberation is still a long way off. In the end, the Church is there only to reinforce the male power syndrome.

The image of God as a man is very deeply entrenched, even in people who have rejected the idea of God: the God we no longer believe in is still envisaged as male. It's hardly surprising, and very convenient for a world ruled by men to see its creator as a man. Where power is equated with masculinity, the most powerful figure must be masculine.[3]

For those feminists who do need involvement in religious worship there is a female avenue open; the growing goddess and priestess cults. The Madrian movement is one such example, incorporating rituals and moon festivals and sacrificial rites (which it is gleefully announced were 'roundly condemned by Jeremiah in the name of his male god in the Old Testament' (Jeremiah 34.15 – 30)).[4]

The aim of this chapter is not to argue against this analysis of Christianity, not to defend the Church, nor to investigate the many worrying aspects of the goddess cults. The final part of the book will be offering an alternative rendering of the impact which Christianity has made on the lives and insights of women. But here we are forced to ask the question: does the Church have a case to answer? Is the Church, along with work, education and family life, guilty of *repressing* women, guilty of denying them true expression of that personhood? To examine this we turn not to the dismissive comments of the majority of feminists but to heartfelt arguments of that much smaller group of women, the feminists within the Church.

Male bias in our churches?
The consensus appears to be that as it is presented and practised in our churches the gospel is not *Good News* for women. After 2,000 years the Church remains an institution structured by men for men. Whilst proclaiming eternal freedom in Christ it endorses temporal bondage for women. Whilst preaching that in Christ there is no male or female it practises the subordination of women to the overruling and authority of men. Whilst maintaining that we are all part of the body of Christ it acts as though the male parts are far more important than the female parts. Women, it is argued, are stifled in the majority of churches. Talented women who love the Lord and want to serve him find the outlets for such service very circumscribed. Women with pastoral, administrative or teaching gifts find in many churches that they must sit back frustrated whilst some man performs very inadequately a task that they would do so much better. For although a number of denominations in the United States in particular do recognize the varieties of ministry for women, on the whole most churches on either side of the ocean see women as playing only a 'supportive', if any, role in their congregations. Men preach, women listen. Men pray, women say 'Amen'. Men form the clergy, the diaconate or the oversight, women abide by their leadership. Men study theology, women sew for the bazaar. Men make decisions, women make the tea. Women's role, even within the Church, is primarily that of wife and mother, and many church people feel very uneasy when a woman moves out of that role into another. Working wives who are very involved in their jobs and not able to take part in the women's groups, in the cleaning rota or the domestic back-up of a church are frequently shown disapproval or hostility. They are seen as somehow more worldly than their domestic counterparts,

even though they might be struggling harder to relate and integrate their Christian faith with their work lives than many mums at home. Similarly, with the swing away from celibacy as the super-spiritual norm, single women often find churches unsympathetic and alienating, with their contemporary focus on the family and their adulation of motherhood. If to be a really successful Christian woman is to be a wife and mother, then surely they have failed on all accounts?

The Church then wants women in their 'normal', 'proper' role. It is happiest with women who are supportive and domestic, women who are uncritical and non-threatening, docile, feminine, good followers, hospitable and passive. Most churches are embarrassed with women who feel called to leadership, women who are perceptive and analytical, women who are learned in Scripture and have developed biblical insights. The best they can do for them is to recognize that if they were men there would be much they could tackle in the Church, but as they are women then they simply constitute a problem. Perhaps the answer might be to get them interested in missionary work. There are, after all, plenty of opportunities for women in Christian service and evangelism if they don't mind going overseas.

Attitudes to women
It is the incongruity of the Church's position on women which offends many feminists. In fact for all its attempted theological justification the way many churches treat women has more to do with contemporary secular culture than biblical teaching. Participation in the life of the Church is often split along the same gender lines as we find in the area of work in general. Women do menial, 'low status' tasks, women spend their time with toddlers and children. Lip service is frequently made to the enormous contribution which women make in these areas, but most people recognize that the contribution made by the minister, the deacons, the church treasurer is altogether of a different value. Churches and denominations of course do differ. In some, women will be found at many different levels of church life, in others, women will be doing the cleaning, catering, sewing, ironing, and crèche and Sunday school duties only. I have been to at least one rigidly segregated church where the men have been at earnest prayer in the main hall, whilst the women bustled

around outside, talking in hushed whispers about inconse-
quentials, and organizing the tea and cakes which followed.
It is not surprising in those cases that women not well
socialized into this tradition feel confused and rebellious.

In most churches the attitude to women is much more
subtly communicated. Mildly sexist jokes from the pulpit are
not only tedious but harmful as they continue to foster
inaccurate stereotypes which prevent true growth in the body.
'Put down' comments, aimed often at keeping women in their
place, are not uncommon if women speak out of turn. Nor is
the patronizing and sometimes paternalist attitude of many
clergymen to a predominantly female congregation. It
effectively distances him from real communication and from
showing his own vulnerability. The labelling and categorizing
of some women—'a busybody', 'miserable looking', 'a do-
gooder', 'a neurotic woman', 'always calling round under
some pretext'—is again not only discourteous but betrays a
lack of love and a hollowness in the Church which often
contribute to the very symptoms complained of. Many women
come away from church, and even from small group meetings
and Bible studies, feeling that they have been preached at,
talked at, lectured to and put in place, but have not been
encountered as real persons, with real human needs and a
longing for deep communication. Women students whose
feminist friends have begun to wrestle with the gospel of
Christ often ask me: '*Where* can we take them, where the
sexist attitudes they hate will not be evident?' The question is
a real one indeed.

Sexist language

The development of language is an absorbing topic for
language is not 'neutral', words and phrases all have meaning
within a framework of communication which reflects the
values and commitments of that society or group. The
language of the seventeenth century, rich in Christian
symbolism, heavy in its consciousness of sin, deeply reflects
a world view where God's righteousness was feared, and his
grace and mercy loved. The language of the late twentieth
century is a language of apostasy: of intense humanist self-
preoccupation, of denial of God and blasphemy. The feminist
argument then, that our language also often reflects the low
position which women are given in our culture, can be easily

understood. The replacement of chair*man*, draughts*man*, spokes*man*, *Mrs*, with more linguistically relevant terms irritated many, but have quickly become commonly adapted into the language of many groups. Unfortunately in our churches language betraying a male orientation is still very evident. The conceptualization of God as male is done through language. God, as we well know from Scripture, is neither male nor female and there are many biblical references which liken him to a mother as well as to a father. Yet it is true that the Church frequently attributes maleness to God instead of recognizing that both maleness and femaleness are derivatively God's image. Worship too is often drenched in male language. Many hymns address the congregation as 'brothers' or 'men': 'O *brothers* lift your voices triumphant songs to raise', 'Join hands then *brothers* of the faith', 'Name him, *brothers,* name him', 'We are the children of thy love, the *brothers* of thy well-beloved son', 'Onward therefore pilgrim *brothers*', 'O *brother* man'. Many Christian women are happily prepared to sing 'Rise up, O *men* of God', or 'Good Christian *men* rejoice' but must feel pretty silly when it comes to 'Our wives, and children we commend to thee'. In a similar way we sing about the 'Faith of our *fathers* living still' and remember that 'In thee our *fathers* trusted and were saved' and 'for the might of thine arm we bless thee, our God, our *fathers'* God'.

The militaristic aspect of many of our hymns is also disconcerting. True, the Christian life is pictured often as a warfare, but this feature almost more than any other seems to have excited the minds of many nineteenth-century hymn-writers. The picture we have is of blood-red banners, fighting soldiers, brandished steel, the fierce battle, defeats of the enemy, and victors' crowns. For most women, this image of the Christian life bears little resemblance to their own, or to anything they have experienced or can identify with.

Exclusion, not just from leadership but from expression in worship itself, leaves many women today asking deep questions about the relevance of the Christian faith to themselves. Some churches are slow to produce answers. One important, and incidentally very loving, group of churches, the Brethren, imply by their very name that there are no women in their assemblies. Indeed, some of the assemblies worship that way also.

Inconsistencies in practice

In defence of the traditional attitude of the Church to women's place within it, it must be said that it is not an attempt merely to propagate male supremacy. People of integrity who have struggled with Scripture and who want to obey the Lord of Scripture have in the end come to the conclusion that this same Scripture teaches the subordination of women to men. The Catholic Church's teaching finds its justification in tradition as much as in the Word of revelation, but its conclusions are not too dissimilar. The argument goes that if the Word (or the Church) comes to this conclusion we have no choice but to obey it. We are under authority. The idea of authority is unpopular in contemporary society; nevertheless Christians at least, and Christian women in particular, must take that stand on the authority of the Word of God and put it into practice.

This argument is of course very compelling. No Christian woman wants to be guilty of flouting divine commands. No truly Christian woman wants to live a life denying the authority of Christ, however hard it may be to accept that authority. Yet this bland assertion of scriptural teaching and the exhortation to obedience hides the fact that hermeneutical principles are involved in understanding Scripture, and that two people who both fully accept the Word of God as authoritative might nevertheless come up with different conclusions about individual doctrines or practices. We have accepted this for many years in the Evangelical community with regard to baptism: whether it is reserved for believers or available to infants. In this case we recognize that there are good biblical arguments on either side, and rather than pursue them at every turn we concentrate on the enormous number of beliefs which unite us: on the Triune God, on salvation through Christ, on the virgin birth, on the miracles, the resurrection, the second coming, on the atonement and justification by faith, on the need for repentance and the unmerited grace of God. In a similar way, we are constantly making allowances and adjustments for fellow and sister believers who see in Scripture something which we have not (yet) seen. Only the arrogant maintain that they have all the truth of Scripture enshrined within their confession. Most recognize that whilst this is what *we* believe, this is where *we* stand, *you* might yet have insights from the Word which we can learn from. Obedience involves humility.

In another sense, we are all making some adjustments and reinterpretations to the teachings of the Word of God in applying them to our contemporary culture. We do not consider the prohibition about eating strangled meat (Acts 13.20, 29) to be relevant to us today. It is true also that only a few congregations meet for worship in the way clearly laid down in 1 Corinthians 14.26 – 36. Many of our denominations would find it difficult indeed to cope with people standing up and prophesying, especially when someone is already on his feet in the pulpit. Throw in three people who speak in a tongue, and those interpreting and we have a situation which would strike terror into the hearts of many clergymen! The approach so often taken is to say this was specific to the first century Church, and not for us today. At the same time many church groups nevertheless abstract verse 36 out of the passage, and insist that women should still remain silent! In fact in this passage Paul is almost certainly aiming to prohibit disruptive noise from the women, who might otherwise break into the worship asking questions. If they have anything to ask they should raise it with their husbands at home. If it were to have the stronger meaning, then Paul's earlier reflections about women praying or prophesying with their heads covered would not make sense. Rather than be concerned with what they wore, he would simply insist that they did not pray or prophesy at all. Some churches in fact 'improve' on Paul here: insisting both that women keep silence, and keep their heads covered! But again, the majority of churches now recognize that the wearing of veils or head coverings was pertinent to that situation and not to today.

Incongruities of this nature multiply in our churches. It is not at all unusual for churches to conclude that whilst a woman may never teach the Word of God to adult congregations (basing this on 1 Timothy) they may nevertheless teach children in Sunday school. A quick reflection will soon recognize that if a woman is unfit to impart truth to those of maturity, reflection and wisdom, it would hardly be wise to allow her free access to the immature, trusting and formative minds of children. Similarly, the disparity between women's ministry at home, and missionary work overseas could well be construed to be making a racist comment. Some denominations are more incongruous than others. In England a woman may teach, preach and train men for the Anglican 'priesthood' at theological college, but may not become a 'priest' herself. Only by a very tortuous process can the 'authority' over the future leaders of the Church whilst in training be less 'authoritative' than the 'authority' of a minister in his parish! The administration of the sacraments is another altogether odd phenomenon, where women ordained as deaconesses traditionally administer the wine, but rarely the bread. Is the blood of Christ of less value than the body? What extra 'spiritual' powers are necessary to administer one rather than the other? In many churches of course, women administer neither, even though nothing at all is mentioned in Scripture prohibiting this.

The only point I am trying to make here is that once we move away from the central doctrinal themes of our faith there is a great deal of debate about the contemporary relevance of other teachings of the New Testament. The Church's task all the time is to separate that which holds for all time from that relative to one culture or period. It is the muddled and compromising way in which the Church does this with relation to women which frustrates many Christian feminists, and leaves the Church often unable to account for the stand it takes.

The ordination of women

It has often been supposed that a discussion of women and the Church is, in the end, about the ordination of women. I hope I have shown that the issues are more complex than that. In fact far from being the central pivot of the debate about women, the ordination of women is predominantly a problem for those only with a high view of the sacraments and ordination itself. Those who see ordination as bestowing a special spiritual status on its recipients, who see 'priesthood' not as something which belongs to all believers but to a special few; they are the ones for whom the question of women in the whole process rages most fiercely. For if women are to be forever excluded from this group of the spiritual élite then they are indeed to be relegated to a permanently lower Christian status than men. They will be the ones denied the 'vocation' of priest; unable to preside over the sacraments; unable to administer the host. They will never be numbered amongst those empowered to mediate between Christ and his people.

This view of the priesthood is of course closest to the Catholic and Anglo-Catholic position. For women with a different concept of the ministry of the Church the issues are also different. For them it is not so much being 'set apart' for the holy calling as being enabled to speak the word of God, without let or hindrance, to their generation. It is the recognition of the Church that God can use women too in the proclamation of his gospel and the furtherance of his kingdom. It is a plea for the recognition that they too have the skills and talents to minister to the people, serve the Church, and pastor and nurture the faith of others.

A third view of ministry is often evident. Many women see their calling as *sharing* ministry with others in the Church. This view is furthest away from the hierarchical concept of the Church, with the popes or archbishops at the top and the laity at the bottom, and closest to one which sees every member of the Church as equally effective in the service of Christ and in the life of the Church, but where some occupy specific 'offices' in the Church for certain periods. Here, the ambition of women in this area is simply to be recognized as possible office-holders alongside men, in a ministry in which all can share and use for the upbuilding of the whole body. This view of 'leadership', although most often found in the more gender-rigid of our churches, is in fact closest to that developed in the women's movement itself.

One area of women's ministry which seems to some to be the worst of both worlds is that of the Anglican deaconess. Ordained along with the men she has trained with she nevertheless does not go on to the 'final ordination' a year later as they do. Moreover, her job in the Church is often misunderstood and full of ambiguities: she is seen as an ecclesiastical social worker, a lay reader, a visitor for the sick, an honorary clergy wife, or as a kind of nun. Even if they value her ministry, everyone in the parish knows that the 'real' clergy are men.

There are therefore many questions prior to the ordination of women. What does ordination mean? In what sense do 'spiritual authority' and church office coincide? To what extent is the sharing pattern of 'equals' in Christ closer to the New

Testament Church than the hierarchy we observe today? It could be that in a curious kind of way the feminist arguments outside the Church might be pointing at something we need to know.

Notes

1. Wendy Collins, Ellen Friedman and Agnes Pivot, *The Directory of Social Change* (Wildwood House 1978), p. 13.
2. Jessie Bernard, *The Female World.* New York, Free Press, 1981.
3. *The Directory of Social Change,* p. 13.
4. ibid., p. 14.

PART TWO
THE FEMINIST DIAGNOSIS

Feminists do not only address themselves to the facts *of inequality and oppression; they want the situation to change. But what to do about oppression depends largely on what is causing it. So it is with the 'why' of inequality that many feminists are primarily concerned and with this concern the widespread agreement about* how *women are unfairly treated becomes a deep and jagged debate about the reasons for it. There are different feminist positions which produce different diagnoses, and thus different remedies for cure. Although many feminists cross theoretical boundaries, it is possible to distinguish three major secular feminist perspectives: liberal feminism and the equal rights tradition, Marxist feminism and its emphasis on the economic and class system, and radical feminism with its attack on patriarchy and the commitment to a woman-centred ideology. In this section we shall look at each of these in turn for a deeper understanding of how they see the root causes of the oppression of women.*

7: Liberal Feminism

The equal rights tradition of the liberal feminists predates modern feminism and comes from a very different ideological home. Although I shall argue later that all three forms of secular feminism share a similar point of departure, the direction travelled by the liberal feminists is somewhat different to that taken, for example, by the Women's Liberation Movement.

Whereas socialist feminists were to concentrate on economic rights as defined by nineteenth- and twentieth-century socialist theory, and radical feminists on sexual rights, as outlined in the twentieth-century sexual liberation theory, liberal feminists have been traditionally concerned about political rights, as defined in eighteenth- and nineteenth-century liberalism. This broad distinction has other implications. Unlike their more radical counterparts liberal feminists have been the ones actively backing legal reforms as an important part of the way ahead. Unlike their more Marxist counterparts liberal feminists have been content to work within the system, hoping that a sounder non-sexist educational programme, along with new legislation, will eventually result in a new freer era for women. There is clearly a kind of optimism inherent in liberal feminism which the other positions do not share. What is it then which makes this perspective distinct and gives it its focus?

John Stuart Mill
It would be no exaggeration to claim that the work of John Stuart Mill (1806—1873) provided the spearhead for this type of feminist thinking. His collusion with Harriet Taylor, their subsequent marriage after the death of her husband and her influence on his own feminism culminated in a series of essays and pamphlets setting out their demands for a reappraisal of the position of women. His main work of this kind was written alone, however, after Harriet Taylor's death. *On the Subjection of Women,* published in 1869, soon became the feminist centrepiece as educated women throughout the world read and discussed it. It had become available in twelve countries and eight languages by 1870. Women's

discussion groups all over Europe focused on this tract and found it irresistible.

Because an examination of Mill's position spells out for us so satisfyingly the chasm which still exists between liberal feminists and a more radical stance it is worth taking the time to do this. For Mill was a liberal theorist *par excellence.* He took his cue from the Enlightenment commitment to the autonomy of the individual and the faith in human reason, to which we shall return later, in chapter fourteen. Then he wedded this individualism to the nineteenth-century belief in self-help, self-discipline, *laissez-faire* and 'morality'. Liberalism contested the 'divine right' of monarchs or aristocrats to rule, but it did not advocate rule of the masses either. Mill saw the majority as mediocre, and feared social collectivities because he saw them as enforcing conformity and mediocrity on the whole society and on the individual. Activity of the state then was to be reduced to a minimum so that the sovereignty of the individual could have full political and economic recognition. This way, all artificial inequalities, all barriers to the free competition of free individuals would be swept away. Eventually, the just, most able, most moral and the 'exceptional' would emerge as leaders who would then use their power not to usurp or dictate but in the interests of all. 'The greatest happiness of the greatest number' summarizes the Utilitarian maxim which Mill espoused.

For some, a belief in the sovereignty of the individual alongside the need for maximizing happiness for all might be an uneasy marriage. To a certain extent it was for Mill. For happiness for the majority means freedom from poverty, good health and a sound diet. Yet liberalist *laissez-faire* means contesting state interference, endorsing private property and inheritance and allowing unregulated freedom of production and exchange. Mill himself wavered on this point, and it was through his reading of Saint-Simon that he moved into a new appreciation of socialism. Yet it was socialism within liberalism. It allowed him to advocate limitations on the system of distribution but to leave almost all other aspects of capitalist society untouched. The fundamental system was never challenged. When we look at his liberal feminism it bears a similar hallmark.

Mill saw the need for a society then where individuals could be free; where the fundamental rights were rights of the citizen, where those 'exceptional' people could transcend mediocrity and supply strong and firm leadership. Where was such a society to be found? Mill had his own choice. Victorian England came as close to the liberal utopia as any country. Yet even here the utopia was not realized. There was one outstanding exception to the freedom of the individual: 'In no instance except this which comprehends half the human race, are the higher social functions closed against anyone by a fatality of birth which no exception and no change of circumstances can overcome'.[1] What is this instance? The situation of the labouring classes? No, it is the position of women. Women alone, it seems, were denied access to the 'higher social functions' irrespective of their merit or ability. Therefore this movement from subjection to full equality for women would for Mill mark the final stage in the development of a perfectly liberal and reasonable society.

It is difficult to imagine that the Victorian England which Mill so readily endorsed with his one exception, was the same Victorian England which Engels had described earlier in his *Condition of the Working Classes.* There is no doubt in fact that Mill's vision was very partial, and he judged society from the position of an able, educated, affluent gentleman. What is more it is clear that the women he had in mind were similarly middle-class, privileged women who would profit from education, entry into the professions, the right to retain an inheritance and so on. Working-class women whose lives would continue to revolve around domestic service, the 'sweated trades' and factory work would hardly find his concept of equality to be one which affected them greatly.

Mill's belief was that with the removal of legal constraints which handicapped women they would begin to experience freedom, becoming self-sufficient and able to direct their own lives. Emancipation or liberation thus meant changing the law, opening up areas of employment, allowing women to own property after marriage, and granting them suffrage and full citizenship. It certainly did not involve one in a discussion of social classes. Yet even here there is an ambiguity. For Mill recognized that it was not individual women who were being denied true citizenship and hence equality but *women as a social group* or, as later critics have claimed, a 'sexual' class. This awareness of structural inequality lifts him out of the traditional liberal mould and immediately makes his stance more radical and more in tune with Engels or Saint-Simon than might otherwise have seemed the case. Yet the radicalism did not extend to any challenging of capitalism or of patriarchy—two systems which both underpinned and defined liberalism. In terms of women's 'natural' role Mill was thoroughly patriarchal. Women were in the end more likely to be happiest at home with children and domestic life. Even though he denied that women had any 'innate nature', and even talked about the 'legal slavery of marriage', he nevertheless remained apparently convinced that this would be and should be the choice of the majority. 'It does not follow that a woman should *actually* support herself because she should be *capable* of doing so: in the natural course of events she will not.' Ideally the husband should be able to earn enough for them both: 'and there would be no need that the wife should take part in the mere providing of what is required to *support* life: it will be for the happiness of both that her occupation should rather be to adorn and beautify it'.[2] He did not argue then that men and women were the same. He conceded it might even be the case that women had quite different psychological needs and faculties from men, although he believed their mental and creative powers to be equal. However, that was not the point for Mill. It was that the *choice* of developing all her abilities and discovering for herself their limitations should be allowed the woman. In the end it could be left to her, and the free play of market forces (the liberal dream) to ensure that she did what she was best fitted for. If women wished to work then there should be no hindrance from the law: 'Whatever women's services are most wanted for, the free play of competition will hold out the strongest inducements for them to undertake.'[3] We shall see later how enormously this contrasts with a Marxist reading of the same situation.

Mill was not only a theorist. As a Member of Parliament he was active in reforms which he saw as the logical outworking of his liberal faith and commitment, especially in campaigns for the legal equality of women. As early as 1865 he was fighting for women's suffrage, sixty-four years before it was fully granted. He even joined the Christian campaigner Josephine Butler in 1871 on the attempted repeal of the Contagious Diseases Act which endorsed so totally the Victorian 'double standard' of sexual morality. Mill, however, came in response to the threat against individual liberty rather than from the Christian position of the campaign leader.

Mill's own attitude to Christianity was interesting. Although he generally approved of Protestantism he remained aloof from Christianity and was more at home in the Unitarian circles in which he moved. Certainly, he frequently endorsed the importance of religion and conscience as vital to the development of morality, but this was to be religion which would be socially and theologically tolerant of all others: Christianity with no teeth. The 'repressive' tendencies of some creeds and churches must be checked. He singled out Calvinism as an example of a repressive and harsh system which narrows human options and threatens individuality: the emphasis on *obedience,* even to God's will, can only stifle human character.[4] From the harshness of his comments on Calvinism it might seem to many that Mill's own tolerant liberal faith was not after all tolerant enough to accept those he did not agree with.

Contemporary liberal feminism and liberal theory

Although Mill's contribution to feminism has been a lasting one and his stance as a legal reformer active on women's behalf was to be echoed by liberal feminists for the next hundred years, his particularly Victorian liberal emphasis has not endured. Few, if any, feminists today would accept liberalism in its full sense of *laissez-faire,* self-help and self-determination. In a very real sense liberal feminist politics have outlived their own theory. The 'freedom of the individual' has a hollow ring when removed from the sound archives of the well-tuned nineteenth-century liberal philosophy. The result is that today liberal feminism has no longer any theory which can inform its political strategy and policies. The basic tenets are still maintained: freedom of choice, equality of opportunity, freedom of competition, the rights of the individual. But this is now the *status quo.* Because liberal values are so thoroughly embedded in our Western societies, because liberalism is now the establishment ideology, it is difficult to be reflective and self-conscious about it. These values have lost their 'specific' identity. They appear as the 'neutral' starting-point: the hidden assumptions behind much political strategy. This is why liberal feminists today rarely discuss a theory of individuality: they themselves are likely to be starting from the same ideology of individualism and competition. Liberal feminists today would still argue that emancipation can be fully achieved without any major alteration to the economic structures of contemporary capitalist democracies. Nor would we expect to find any major challenge to the patriarchal system from 'mainstream' liberal feminism. For the problem is not with systems *per se* — class or patriarchal. It remains at a deep level to be one of individual freedom: freedom which can be denied in any economic or political system unless measures are introduced which will counteract this. The fact that liberalism has not yet produced a 'society of equals' envisaged by Mill is no indication that the liberal faith and vision have failed: it simply means they have not yet been fully applied.[5]

Liberal feminism in the twentieth century

It is usually argued that feminist activity in this century is divided into two periods. Up to and into the 1920s agitation from women's pressure groups was effective in producing enormous changes in the legal, political and educational status of women. This period is regarded by many as the heyday of liberal feminism. In the two years from 1918 to 1920 women had been enfranchised in Britain, Germany, Austria, Netherlands, Poland, the United States and the USSR.

By 1925 women had been admitted to jury and magistrate service in Britain and the US, joined the police force, had entered the British parliament and been admitted to the professions. They had formed part of the delegation at the League of Nations, been granted degrees at Oxford University, been given maintenance after divorce and equal guardianship of infants. In 1922 a woman won election to the judiciary of the Ohio State Supreme Court. In 1923 the ERA was first introduced into the American Congress and the British Trade Union Congress was chaired by a woman for the first time. It was indeed a heady period and the liberal dream seemed realizable.

Yet this activity did not persist. Although liberal feminists were still evident between 1930 and 1960, for the campaign for women's equality they were lean years. To start with, the Great Depression was hardly the time for women to focus on their rights. Then the Second World War complicated the issue. Suddenly women's work was needed as never before. Massive propaganda campaigns were launched in both Britain and the US encouraging women to put their country before themselves. The home, it seemed, was no longer the only place to bring up a family. Government-sponsored crèches and day nurseries could apparently provide as happy an environment for a small child as any living room or kitchen. Women could adapt themselves to munitions work as easily as to a sewing machine. Many women thus threw in their lot with the war effort and began to experience advantages of being wage-earners, and visible contributors to the nation's security. Yet with the end of the War and the return of the men these newly developed work roles abruptly ceased. Day nurseries were closed, women's skills were no longer wanted and the propaganda now focused on the neglectful working mother who did not realize that her place was, after all, in the home. Of course, many of the women needed little persuasion. For those who had been *required* to work for their country, liberation meant having the freedom to stay at home and enjoy a domestic role. Yet there were others who felt they had been *used* by the government machinery: dragged into the labour force when the country depended on them, but discarded without compensation as soon as possible after-wards. But the 1950s was the decade of the domestic woman, the decade of rebuilding, of population growth, of affluence. For many feminists it seemed also to be the decade of complacency.

Beneath the calmness, however, a massive sea-swell was slowly developing. Deeply submerged anger meant the next wave of feminism which broke on to the unprepared beaches of the 1960s had gathered with it so much pent up force and energy that it threatened to wash away the patriarchal structures which resisted it. Nor did this new feminism have many words of comfort for the old style liberal feminist stance. The radicals were not slow to dismiss it as 'bourgeois feminism' claiming that it 'concentrated on the more superficial symptoms of sexism — legal inequalities, employ-ment discrimination and the like'.[6]

The impression often given, now, is that liberal feminism had really petered out by the end of the 1960s and has not emerged significantly since. The utopia of the freedom of the individual, brought about through changes in legislation ensuring a more egalitarian system, has not and cannot be realized. Thus the radical stance of the sixties and seventies was necessary to sweep away reformist ideas and for the movement to come of age. Yet it would be quite misleading to suggest that the advent of the feminism of the far left heralded the demise of liberal feminism and the equal rights tradition. In fact, throughout this period they were equally as active as their more radical sisters. An interesting repercussion of the high publicity given to the demands for women's liberation at this time was the additional weight it gave not to the new radicals, but to the old liberals. What is more, the deeper feminist fervour brought new blood into the liberal camp and invigorated many campaigns. It is also true that many of the legislative issues enacted in the 1960s were as a result of activity carried out before the radicals ever hit the scene. Many of these new measures were rejected as too demanding, but general consciousness had now been raised to the level where the suggestions of the liberals no longer seemed as far-fetched as they had a decade ago. The American Equal Pay Act in 1963 was a definite product of liberal feminist activity, as were the British Equal Pay Act of 1970 and the Sex Discrimination Act of 1975. So the sixties and seventies saw consolidation and development of many programmes. The old generation of liberal feminists remained at work in Congress and in Parliament but now with more support at grass roots and a larger movement behind them.

Whilst in the US the distinction between radical and liberal stayed quite pronounced during this period, in Britain there was much blurring of the edges. Although three positions could be found they were not always represented by different groupings. Women's groups in the Labour Party, for example, although in many senses still in the liberal feminist tradition with accent on legislation, would also include women much further to the left and those who adopted a more radical stance. Single campaigns tended to draw feminists of all perspectives together. The pro-abortion campaign of the 1960s was one such issue culminating in the Abortion Law of 1968. Yet the support was still not unanimous, even here. Many of the older generation of liberal feminists argued that abortion was not part of the feminist case. Edith Summerskill, the Labour MP, was one such example. As a public supporter of birth control since 1935 when she had faced hostility from many in her constituency, she felt abortion was a retrogressive step in the women's programme. A long-term champion of the rights of housewives she also vehemently opposed the changes in the divorce laws which became effective in 1971, on the grounds that they were a 'Casanova's charter'. They would give a green light to male desertion and leave many women undefended and unsupported.[7]

Betty Friedan

For many, the most influential contemporary feminist in the liberal camp has been Betty Friedan. Her book *The Feminine Mystique* (1963) and the subsequent National Organization for Women (NOW) in 1966 spoke to a mass audience. She focused on the 'traditional' woman: the mother and the housewife. Her style was powerful and her many lectures very persuasive. Her message reached women where they were. One of the targets for her attack was Freudian psychology and the way it reinforced the traditional role of women whilst infusing them with guilt about their own inadequacies and failings as mothers. Her own diagnosis was simple: women were discontent, not because they were not given enough training as housewives and mothers but because being a housewife was *intrinsically boring.* It was the way women lost their individual identity; their potential was crippled into the roles of wife and mother. Individuality was stifled, real personhood denied and true choice not offered. The (male) cultural definition of femininity, the 'feminine mystique', defined for women what they should be. Betty Friedan's ambition, then, was to free women from destructive dependence produced in them by the patriarchal culture.

In many ways this sounds very radical. Yet there was so much which Betty Friedan did not challenge. She was not drawn into any deeper analysis of the patriarchal system which provided the context for these traditional roles. Nor did she offer any critique of liberalism as a distinct political ideology. Instead she adopted a 'liberal rights' theory: a theory stressing the need for equality through political action. Individual self-fulfilment remained the goal, realizable through greater education for women, legal reform and bringing women into the public arena: 'It is the *right* of every woman in America to become all she is capable of becoming on her own, or in partnership with a man.'[8]

The radical critique of this approach will be examined in depth later. It is enough here to note that the most fundamental objection is that it accepts a liberal pluralism as its starting-point: it wants women to be represented as an interest group in the political decision-making process. Instead of a critique which challenges what the radicals see as the very basis of sexism in society she instead accepts the system as given, and tries to gain a better place for women within it. In fact Betty Friedan's position becomes increasingly more liberal and less radical as the years pass. By 1979 she is implicitly almost challenging her own position of 1963. She begins to argue that although the 'feminine mystique' still limits and squeezes the potential of women, it has changed. No longer is it simply that of identifying women with their roles of housewife and mother. It is also that of the working woman. The trends of the previous decade had drawn women into the market, into public life certainly, but a new kind of slavery had replaced the old. 'Why should women simply replace the glorification of domesticity with the glorification of work as their life and identity?'[9] But is this not what the liberal feminists had been working for — to open up these very avenues for women? If they had, then for Betty Friedan it now revealed new dangers, new problems and still at a deep level no freedom for women. In a sense this new departure was parallel to the radical critique. She was challenging the concept of equality which simply produced women who were identical to their male counterparts. Now she wanted women to be identified with their specific and feminine contribution. Yet this is not a woman-centred analysis in quite the same way as that advocated by many radical feminists. For it also involves abandoning many of the radical positions which by now had been adopted by the National Organisation for Women. She asks poignantly: 'Must the women's movement for equality come into ultimate conflict with the profound values of life that, for me as for others, have always been associated with women?'[10] The outcome then is to draw back from a radical position on 'sexual politics', which she claimed had in any case alienated and threatened many people and held up the movement for real equality. Women should still be free to choose abortion or any other aspect of their individual needs and rights, but abortion should certainly not be widely advocated or hold centre-stage. The emphasis likewise on rape, incest, and lesbianism should be abandoned, and instead there should be a rediscovery of the values which *linked people together* in community. Man-hatred had no place in this programme: co-operation and partnership between the sexes should be stressed. The family in particular should be reappraised in the light of the anonymity and impersonality of society. Far from dismissing the family as reactionary we should begin to recognize it as

the symbol of that last area where one has any hope of individual control over one's destiny, of meeting one's most basic human needs, of nourishing that core of personhood threatened now by vast impersonal institutions and uncontrollable corporate and government bureaucracies and the bewildering, accelerating pace of change.[11]

Where does this leave liberal feminism? To a certain extent it leads them back into traditional liberalism and further away from a radical analysis. Yet Betty Friedan's latest analysis simply reflects the variety of opinion amongst feminists today. Certainly not all liberal feminists would agree with her. Many of the British activists would be only marginally affected by such writings, feeling there is still a long way to go before we have the luxury of this kind of reflection. Radical American feminists regard this as the logical outcome of her position all along and a movement further into a bourgeois liberalism. Nevertheless, in spite of her uncritical starting-point, Betty Friedan has hit upon a very important issue: the endurance of and the need for the family. Yet her solution is only withdrawal — a creation of a safe haven of privacy and peace in an anonymous, hostile, public world. Whilst the Marxists challenge the ostrich mentality of this, and the radicals the patriarchal bourgeois acceptance of heterosexuality, Christians will recognize her solution to be going in the right direction — but from the wrong basis.

Notes

1. J. S. Mill, *On the Subjection of Women.*
2. Friedrich H. Hayek, *J. S. Mill and Harriet Taylor: Their Friendship and Subsequent Marriage* (Routledge and Kegan Paul 1951), p. 65.

3. J. S. Mill, *On the Subjection of Women;* quoted in Richard Evans, *The Feminists* (Croom Helm 1979), p. 221.
4. J. S. Mill, *On Liberty.*
5. A good critique of liberal feminism is to be found in Zillah Eisenstein, *The Radical Future of Liberal Feminism,* Longman 1981.
6. Shulamith Firestone, *Dialectic of Sex: The Case for Feminist Revolution* (New York, Bantam, 1970), p. 32.
7. Olive Banks, *Faces of Feminism* (Oxford, Martin Robertson, 1981), pp. 187, 198, 240.
8. Betty Friedan, 'Our Revolution is Unique' in M. C. Thomas (ed.) *Voices of the New Feminism* (Boston, Beacon, 1970), p. 34.
9. Betty Friedan, 'Feminism takes a New Turn' *(New York Times Magazine* 18 November 1979), p. 98; quoted by Eisenstein, p. 189.
10. Betty Friedan, *The Second Stage* (New York, Summit Books, 1981), p. 165.
11. ibid., p. 229.

8: Marxist Feminism

Early socialist feminism

It is easy to be misled about the socialist tradition in feminism. All too often it is seen solely as a by-product of the student unrest and civil rights movement of the 1960s. And of course, contemporary Marxist feminism does have this origin. Yet the wider socialist concern for the emancipation of women goes back way beyond this period, and even beyond Marx himself. In fact it too has its roots in the Enlightenment. The ideas of Robert Owen and Saint-Simon which directed this kind of feminism were Enlightenment ideas, starting from the same faith in human autonomy. However, in one important sense they parted from the earlier Enlightenment thinkers: they did not embrace individualism. Instead this basic article of faith was replaced by a belief in the *community,* the social collectivity which would produce the new harmony. It was these ideas then which found their way into early socialist feminism.

By 1826 Anna Wheeler and William Thompson were putting forward socialist doctrines of co-operation and community alongside demands for an end to the economic and political inequalities between the sexes. Thompson's *Appeal of One Half of the Human Race* went further than the demands for an improvement in women's legal and educational position. Principles of co-operation, not competition, were stressed, an end to men's sexual abuse and domination was urged, and a plea made for equal rights in marriage. In this he was very much in the Owenite tradition.

As early as 1812, Owen had been propounding very radical ideas about marriage and the family. Unlike the later liberal theorists, he saw social structures, family upbringing and environment as far more significant than any 'sovereignty' the individual might have. His own outlook was decidedly determinist: in the deepest sense people were not 'free' to choose. 'The character of man is without a single exception always formed for him . . . it may be, and is, chiefly created by his predecessors . . . man never did, nor is it possible he ever can, form his own character.'[1] The family unit then is not a mere given in society; it is rather the conveyor of an ideology, the reinforcer of a socially-constructed state of affairs. The family is in fact the bastion of private property, the propagator of individualist competition and self-interest. Without the traditional family these bastions would fall. Not yet advocating the abandonment of marriage altogether, and certainly not embracing the quite permissive attitudes of Charles Fourier, Owen did believe in easily-available divorce. This must in itself have sounded alarming enough, coming as it did, forty years before the first divorce act. But it was the community model—the social, egalitarian, co-operative replacing the traditional family—which was to be put into practice in the decades which followed.

Owen's own factory in New Lanark and the New Harmony Community were two practical illustrations of his ideas. A more radical view of community grew out of a visit to New Harmony by Fanny Wright, a Scottish-American. An ardent feminist, and already publicly speaking on women's rights in America by 1828, Frances Wright sought to establish a total colony which brought together men, women and children including freed slaves into a single community. The colony was to stand for abolition of slavery, for women's emancipation, for atheism and for socialism. It was a very radical utopia, but one which turned sour as it became discredited through permissive sexual relations and new forms of exploitation replacing the old. The humanist vision proved too optimistic about the inherent goodness of human beings.

The thrust behind these and many other short-lived communities was the abolition of all power relationships. The exploitation of workers by capitalists, of women by men, of children by parents was to be removed. Domination and subordination, power and oppression had no place in the 'New Moral World' of the 1830s and 1840s. This then was no tinkering with the legal framework, whilst keeping capitalist structures intact. Nor was it economic upheaval alongside an acceptance of the personal as 'private'. These early socialists saw their vision as extending to large areas of society: economic, sexual, personal and political. The vision was for total transformation: a new world order.

Early Marxism
It is interesting to note how traditional and unradical Marx himself remained, compared with those who had gone before

him. Neither he nor Engels had any concept of what Shulamith Firestone was later to call the 'sex class'. Sexuality belonged to the personal area. It was the societal area (alone) which needed to be changed. Certainly Engels accepted monogamous marriage as very important, although he felt it did have the drawback of reinforcing private property in the hands of the male. The very nature of sex-love was for Engels necessarily exclusive — 'open' sexual relations would be regressive rather than an improvement. What needed to be improved was the way love had been distorted by capitalism and the way sex had been made a commodity. Similarly, his views on homosexuality would be very unpopular amongst many socialist feminists today. For him, homosexuality was degrading, unnatural, gross and full of vice.[2]

Even though there were feminists among Marx's followers — his own daughter Eleanor being, of course, a noted one — on the whole nineteenth-century Marxism was not noted for its espousal of the cause of women. The fact that most Marxists were uninterested in, if not directly opposed to, women's suffrage has often been interpreted as proof of its inherent sexism. However, this is not entirely fair. Marx and Engels were not excited by *any* suffrage campaigns. They put no hope in reformist ideas and saw enfranchisement of women *or* of the working class as nothing more than further ways of propping up the capitalist system. Nevertheless, we would not have to look far for anti-feminist statements from their followers if we wished to find them. Hyndman, a leading Marxist in Britain for many years, was quite clear that socialism and feminism were not to be united. 'I do not want the movement to be a depository of old cranks, humanitarians, vegetarians, anti-vivisectionists, arti-crafties and all the rest of them; we are scientific socialists and have no room for sentimentalists. They confuse the issue.'[3] It is possible to see then why many later Marxist feminists felt uneasy about identifying too closely with Marx and his earlier followers.

Reformism and the Marxists
Similarly, in retrospect, feminists are not united in their interpretation of the suffragette movement. Whilst identifying with the struggles and sufferings of the suffragettes and their singlemindedness in working for women, there is a deep pessimism as to what in the end they have achieved. Their

vision is seen as only partial: as wanting for women the same citizen rights achieved by men, citizenship as conferred by the right to vote. Yet if women's lives remain structured and controlled by a minority of economically powerful people who lie beyond the ballot box, what use is a vote?

There is a similar ambivalence with regard to the early Labour Party in Britain whose ranks included many of the suffragette workers. Whilst undoubtedly committed to socialism, it saw the means of achieving economic and political equality to be through reformism. Even though many in the left wing of the Labour Party have theoretically embraced a much more radical socialism, the Party as a whole has chosen to work *with* the capitalist system rather than against it. Wider franchise, redistribution of income, social welfare benefits, provision of council housing and a national health service all chipped away at the divide between rich and poor, between 'capitalist' and worker, between those with private property and those without. Yet contemporary Marxists would argue that the chippings have not amounted to much, and the block has been left very largely intact. Power, privilege, wealth and control are still concentrated in the hands of a minority. Reformist socialism has not produced the goods, either for the workers or women. All the Labour Party has done is to soften the blow, creating a paternalist, centralized state run by the middle classes. But the liberal, individualist, competitive, capitalist state emerges as solidly and as powerfully as ever when a right-wing government resumes office.

Women suffer particularly, argue the feminists, under an administration of the right. For part of the new right mentality is to reassert the traditional role of women, irrespective of changing circumstances or of individual needs. In a short time a single administration can undo decades of reformist activity: it can drop the ERA from its platform, it can claw back maternity leave provisions, it can leave a health service starved of funds, it can modify existing legislation to make it ineffective, it can nullify the effect of child benefit schemes. Reformism is no answer to this kind of power. The whole of the political and economic structure needs to be changed.

Marxism and feminism

Marxist feminism, along with the other feminist positions,

was given a fresh infusion in the 1960s when women active in the civil rights movement and the New Left began asking questions concerning the oppression of women, as well as about the oppression of blacks. Since then, both gender and race have become Marxist preoccupations in addition to the traditional one of class. However, an interest in gender did not emerge immediately. The chauvinist attitudes of the men in the New Left in a real sense triggered off a new feminist departure, and one which no longer looked to Marx for its inspiration.

Nevertheless there are feminists who have stayed loyal to the Marxist position even if this has involved them in a radical critique of traditional Marxist views concerning women. Neo-Marxism does not attempt to venerate every word of the founder, but takes the principles of his analysis of class exploitation into wider contemporary areas. Being faithful to Marxism, however, does not merely involve employing left-wing techniques and concepts, such as consciousness-raising, sisterhood, oppression and the like. It involves giving a reason for the *cause* of injustice, inequality and oppression which is in keeping with Marx's own analysis. It involves also maintaining the impossibility of real feminism without socialism, and thus putting the struggle for socialism first.

What then is this Marxist-feminist diagnosis? Clearly, it is not one which puts any weight on individual freedom. To assert the primacy of freedom where structures of inequality make that freedom impossible is whistling in the wind. Any individualist answer is one which *ipso facto* fails to look below the surface of the problem. No, the reason for the oppression of women is at root the same as the reason for the oppression of men. It is the class struggle, the concentration of power into the hands of a few, the ability of a minority to manipulate the majority like pawns on a chess-board. Women, the blacks, the underprivileged, the weak and the working class are together caught in the class trap. They are subdued, divided, and made to compete for scarce resources so that their minds will be on the competition rather than on the much bigger question of why the resources are so scarce. They are used as fodder for the labour market—acting as a reserve army of labour and pulled into active service when the demands of capital need more workers, but discarded when profits fall. Far from Mill's 'free play of competition', it is the manipulation of firms and employees in the interest of profits which directs the use of the work-force. A reformist state might halt or amend this process for a while, but a right-wing government will give more power to the manipulators and less to the workers.

The traditional structures of society—family, Church and school—all serve to support the class ideology. The Church, organized by a professional élite, offers cheap ways of conforming to middle-class values. Education is presented as a ticket for success or a process of failure. Wives are taught to accept low status work as normal. Workers are surrounded by institutions piping out the same message as background music. The Establishment has many voices, all of which serve to lull us into a state of false consciousness, and unthinkingly men and women take on board the same ideology.

What needs to happen therefore is that people are awakened to their true condition, that their consciousness is raised. Once eyes are opened then people will actively work for what is undoubtedly in their own interest. Class identities will be solidified, new demands made, and the tight control which capital exerts over all our lives will start to move.

Class and gender

Although a Marxist analysis of class and oppression is easy enough to understand at this basic level, it is not always clear how this can offer a meaningful analysis of the specific inequalities of women in relation to men. If women and men are united in the class struggle, then why does it seem to be women who are paid less, have fewer employment and promotion opportunities, inferior education, less free time and often considerable family responsibilities? Why is it that the conflict so often seems to be between men and women, if it is really between capital and labour?

The answer would be again on several levels. Marxist feminists would not deny that there is often real conflict between the sexes, just as there is conflict of union against union or miner against miner. But these are pseudo-conflicts, brought about by the manipulations of the capitalist system. Because capital controls our labour, we are made to compete with one another. To understand this fully we need to look at an earlier pattern. Many feminists claim that before the advent of capitalism there was not this same competition and conflict between the sexes. Pre-industrial days are painted with a generous brush which stresses the co-operation in work, the communal living arrangements, and the interdependence of men and women in the work process. The work of both women and men was essential: together they would be at work in the fields, with the animals and livestock, reaping the harvest and sowing the seed. Where division of labour occurred it was not always along gender lines, and did not bring with it any hierarchy or superiority. It was only with industrialization and the development of the capitalist system that these relations changed. The home and the workplace were separated, the men became the wage earners, and the women underwent domestication, and became dependents. With families to *support,* rather than to work alongside in production, the male workforce would be easily controllable and profits for the owners could direct the rhythm of industry.

Of course there are many criticisms of this model, some of which will form the basis of our next chapter. It has been documented elsewhere that an unreasonably rosy glow has been given to pre-industrial work relationships. The main problem is that they fail to take into account the many other aspects of work and life which might modify the argument. For even though women and men certainly worked alongside each other as equals, they were not equal in any other sense. Spinning and weaving were carried out in the home together, but the women did the more menial spinning. Work was family based, *and* the man was very much the head of his family. What is more, a single woman, in Britain at least, if not in the developing American colony, could barely subsist on her own. If she remained unmarried she would most likely join the household of another man where her labour would be important, certainly, but her privileges might well not be those of the blood-related family. Since marriage itself was hardly a matter of choice for the woman, and frequently had simply to do with the size of her goat or pig, her equality in the production process was, in many senses, marginal. The inequality of women certainly predates capitalism.

Most Marxist feminists, however, are not wanting to claim that women's oppression *began* with capitalism, any more than Marx himself claimed that the oppression of slaves and workers began with capitalism. No, the division between exploiters and exploited is to be found in every era of history. The history of society is the history of class struggles. Women themselves have similarly been oppressed in all societies — Greek, Roman, Barbarian, feudal. But the form which the oppression takes is different in each one. It is even different between the major groups in each culture. One of the interests of Marxist feminists is to look at the history of women's oppression, and to document the changes and variations. What is more, they do not claim that this oppression disappears under socialist regimes. Juliet Mitchell, herself a Marxist, concedes that socialist countries as well as capitalist ones have not liberated women. But there is one very emphatic difference: 'The oppression of women is *intrinsic* to the capitalism system — as it is *not* to the socialist.'[4] Under capitalism, then, women's oppression is 'structurally necessary', and only, therefore, if we bring about a 'transformation' of all these structures can women become liberated.

To test this idea we need now to look in some detail at some of the central structures which need this transformation. In doing so we shall be relying heavily on the work of Juliet Mitchell and Sheila Rowbotham, two of the British spokeswomen for contemporary Marxist feminism.

Production and reproduction

Even though, broadly speaking, the word 'production' refers to the means by which we gain control over the creation, in Marxist terminology it is usually tied in with the economy. Involved in the production processes is the division of labour. In *Women's Estate* Juliet Mitchell shows how the different positions which men and women occupy within this division of labour might seem to have been based, throughout history, on the *biological* differences of the sexes. Man's physical superiority has given him the strength to perform arduous kinds of work, whereas woman's physical weakness has taken her out of many forms of labour. However, if this were really the case then capitalism and industrialization would surely have ensured equality in the work process, since machinery could now be used to replace physical power. Yet equality did, manifestly, not appear. Maybe more therefore is involved than mere differences in biology. Sheila Rowbotham takes up the same theme. The division of labour along gender lines is clearly not natural, not a 'given', but is in fact part of the political and economic process. Under capitalism women are doubly exploited in this process: 'Women enter commodity production, and, like men, produce goods which circulate as commodities; they thus share the exploitation and experience of alienation of male workers in capitalism.'[5] Women then, as *part of the working class* are exploited. But there is more to it than that: 'Within the social division of labour in capitalism the task of maintaining and reproducing commodity producers is largely given to women.'[6] *In this process too,* according to Rowbotham and Mitchell, women are also exploited; 'Reproduction in our society is often a kind of sad mimicry of production. Work in a capitalist society is an alienation of labour in the making of a social product which is confiscated by capital.'[7] In a similar way the product of production—the child—becomes a commodity. He will be part of the next generation of workers, necessary for the capitalist system to survive. Capitalism thus has an entrenched interest in the reproductive role of women.

'Reproduction' here does not merely mean giving birth to children. It encapsulates the whole ideology of motherhood, and as such involves all the tasks normally associated with being a mother. Child-bearing, child-rearing, housework, cooking, all are incorporated into this concept of 'reproduction'. It is assumed that because women have children they are somehow better fitted to perform all these other activities also, and so the ideology endures. However, there is a more sinister reason for its endurance according to these writers. It endures because these activities are essential to the operation of capitalist economy. The perpetual requirement of an economy based on profit is that the cost of labour, and the costs of servicing the labouring population, are kept as low as possible. To foster the ideology that the 'natural' place for woman is in the home can only be beneficial for the capitalist enterprise.

In this complex relationship of woman to the processes of production and reproduction can be found the crucial element of difference between her and man, and from there the root of her oppression. For Juliet Mitchell it forms part of a causal chain: 'maternity, family, absence from production and public life, sexual inequality'.[8] For some liberal feminists the answer might seem relatively easy: break one of the links in the chain. Break the connection between motherhood and family, and absence from production. Take women out of the 'private' and into the 'public' arena. For the Marxist feminist however this is no answer. It simply means women 'move to a class-conscious position behind their men'. Entry into the work force is not enough. If it had been, then the fact that 40 per cent of the British labour force is now formed of women would have ensured their equality. But we have seen already that women's position at work more often than not reflects an even greater inequality in terms of wages, conditions and security than that of the 'working classes' in general. Juliet Mitchell sums up the problem: 'The simple entry of women into the labour force in massive numbers, whether under socialism or capitalism, cannot substantially alter the position. Denied the possibility of economic independence . . . women's participation as a huge sector of the working class force remains merely a painful and arduous formality.'[9] In the end, what is necessary is not only a change in patterns of behaviour and life style, nor even a change in ideologies of motherhood — although that would certainly help. Social inequalities including the oppression of women cannot be overcome until the very system of production is changed, and until the key structures which dominate gender differences, those of production and reproduction, are transformed.

Public and private

A distinction which has appeared frequently in this analysis so far is that between 'public' and 'private' and we now need to examine it in some detail. It is very much connected with the Marxist general view on the polarization of the home and the workplace, and is a distinction necessary for the 'structured inequality' to take place. Interestingly, radical feminists make use of the same terms in their own explanation, although, as we shall see, the emphasis is different.

Basically, the argument is that two independent and separate spheres have been created: the *public* world of work, business, politics, institutional religion, education, and the *private* world of family, home, children, sexuality. The public world encompasses institutions which are linked together: links exist between firms, between the economic and political structures, between education and business, between the economy and the military. The public economy is inter-connected, and the rest of the public world revolves around it. The private world, however, is isolated in this process. Households certainly are linked with the public economy and are essential as consumers and reproducers. But they remain private units with no system of exchange amongst themselves. The public world, then, is the world of men, the private world the world of women. However, even in the private world the *power* has not been that of the woman.

To understand the weight given to this distinction we need to return to the pre-industrial period. For here, although a woman's influence beyond domestic life was minimal, domestic life itself incorporated so much more than it came to do after the growth of capitalism. As we have seen, the household was a production unit, and women as co-producers were thus part of the 'public' area of work. Yet this was to be changed; the home became separated from the workplace. Rather than being the place which produces goods to sell in the market, the household became the place which produced labour to sell in the workplace, and for the profit of others. At first, of course, it was the combined labour of the whole family, 'sold' to a single employer as initially the family went *en bloc* into the factory. But after the various Factory Acts it became the labour of the men and boys, who left the home to go to work. Wives and children stayed at home, and the women would perform the non-waged tasks of 'reproduction' which we have just discussed. And so the home became a place unassociated with real work, because money was not earned by housework.

The two realms of home and work were not entirely separated of course, because many women brought paid work into the home. Ways of earning money in the home in the nineteenth century were very varied: childminding, providing lodgings, taking in washing, needlework, hatmaking and, before the regulation of asylums, 'lunatic-keeping'. But this was all invariably very poorly paid. It was not really 'work'; it was done away from the workplace. A similar ambiguity existed with domestic service. For here workers were being brought into the home, to ensure that the middle-class 'housewife' really did have no work to do. Many writers have pointed out that the first women who rushed to call themselves 'housewives' were the very ones who did no housewifery.

So far we have been focusing on the division between home and workplace. But the division between public and private, although for the Marxist relying on this prior distinction, is not identical with it. For the public—private dichotomy involves more than the spatial distance of two realms. The *ideological* distinction in the end was to be more important. People *believed* certain things about the home, and woman's place in it. They *believed* in the home-as-haven, as shelter from the public world; they *believed* in the non-work status of housework; they *believed* in the necessity of mother, not father, to be with children, they *believed* in the privacy of relationships in the home. These beliefs, this 'ideology' has remained constant for more than a hundred years and, the radical feminists will argue, has been responsible for a great deal of abuse in the home, which has been, until recently, largely beyond the (public) law. The Marxist feminists have another problem with these ideas. They are at heart class-based. A non-working wife, and a private home life, became a yearned-for status symbol in the early industrial period. 'Respectability' meant having the means to support a wife in idleness. It meant being able to buy for her the labour necessary to free her from all kinds of work, and present her as the jewel of the household. Much fascinating work has been done showing how even fashions for women during this time reflected this ideology: with some of the undergarments many women would scarcely be able to walk, let alone scrub floors. The freedom of a woman to be *totally domestic* was thus established as a norm, but being domestic involved, of course, doing no work. Nor in fact did ladies spend all their time with their children, since work connected with them also was removed on to the shoulders of others.

The ideal of the private and domestic wife was thus established, and became the definition of womanhood. This meant it was also an ideal for the working classes. Unfortunately, of course, for them this ideal was largely unrealizable, because these women were largely employed in making sure the ideal worked for others. What is more, it has always been unrealizable for that group of women. Working-class women have almost always worked at some stage of their lives, but they have often worked in the 'private' domain of the home. The ideology has been so strong, however, and so persistent that those who have been drawn back into the workplace, into production and out of the private home have often done so with feelings of guilt. Even in studies carried out over the last fifteen years women have confessed to feeling frustrated that they could not fulfil the desired role of being 'just a housewife'. Yet rarely do such women work for their own interests. Even here it has been for the *sake* of the private domain—for their family and home—that they have become wage-earners: accepting exploitation and low pay in order to achieve the ideal of a good, well-provided, well-established haven of rest.

The home ideal itself is also attacked by Marxist feminists. For what is a 'haven of rest' for some is for others a workhouse. The housewife labours, but not in the public arena. No one buys the things she produces. The products of her labour are consumed directly by those in the household. Her work plays no part in government statistics: it is not represented in the Gross National Product. Her labour in fact goes unnoticed by the rest of society, and often by the rest of her family. If she is deserted or abandoned her work leaves her with no skills which she can usefully employ in the public world. Yet her work is essential, a mainspring of the whole economy, but *the public world acts as though it did not exist.* The ideology of the public—private, then, suits capitalism, but it oppresses women.

Marxism and the family

We can sense already that the widely accepted understanding of the family is going to come under strong attack from Marxist feminists. And indeed it does. Their resistance to this model combines the old Owenite faith in community with the Marxist critique of the capitalist-constructed family. The first criticism hits against the idea that the present form of family structure is some kind of natural 'given', and insists instead that it is merely a creation of the capitalist economy. This realization is all the more hidden from the view of the majority because the 'sanctity' and 'privacy' of the nuclear family have been endorsed by successive governments, by the churches and by educational institutions alike. The ideology of this nuclear family: a monogamous unit with a number of offspring living in a semi-detached house, handing on the values of society, but otherwise minding its own business, has thus been given divine, social and political approval; yet in the end, this arrangement is merely one that suits the controlling power structures in society.

Some Marxists are particularly unhappy about the part played by the Church in legitimating the bourgeois family, and see it as one of the ways in which the Church has merely been used as a political tool of capitalism. The typical family of the Bible was in fact not monogamous but polygamous, not nuclear but extended. Even in the New Testament, where monogamy did become the norm, the nuclear family was still not in great evidence. Instead communal living was practised, with approval, and a variety of household forms was in evidence. Why then should the churches see anything 'sacred' in the present pattern? In fact, why endorse it at all unless the Church itself is another pawn of the capitalist system?

The idea of this natural, given family is thus misleading, they argue. In fact, in *most* cultures monogamy is the exception rather than the rule, and a large number of societies practise polygamy. To look at such societies would do much to enlighten our own understanding. For not only do they provide a challenge to the myth of the 'natural', but it is possible to see more clearly how polygamous household arrangements offer an intricate outworking of the processes of production, consumption and the provision of labour. The economic structure of society is thus mirrored in the form of the household. Yet many cannot see that the same is true of western capitalism. Instead the family is seen as being based on affective relations. Of course, this may in part be true, but it masks the much deeper point that it is also the most effective unit for the capitalist system. The family is actually just one means of organizing socio-economic relationships. 'It is not, as has so often been claimed, some kind of "natural", instinctive and sacred unit.'[10]

The capitalist reorganization of the family, the spatial and ideological separation of home and workplace, has brought with it yet other factors. The sex-structured labour market we outlined in part one, the marginal position of women, and the ideology of motherhood have made sense traditionally in the demands for a 'family wage'. The male breadwinner is to be paid enough to support his wife and children. Again, however, we have the myth and the reality. Men in certain classes in society get a family wage, but the rest do not. Yet the concept of a family wage itself carries with it undesirable consequences. Not only does it reinforce the pay structure of industry along gender lines, and thereby enormously deprive the working woman without a male breadwinner; it also perpetuates the financial dependence of women, and the 'degrading aspects of a struggle over the distribution of the wage within the family'.

The Marxist historical analysis has much to offer in its account of the movement from woman-as-producer to woman-as-dependent. Because for the Marxist economic dependence is the most crucial form of dependence, and economic power gives control, the family structure which exists within capitalism — the structure of production and reproduction — ensures a subordinate place to women. This is reinforced by the public/private division where women's occupation of the private realm guarantees their marginality. Similarly, women's work within the family is seen as non-work, it is seen as inferior to that of the breadwinner, it is taken for granted, it is unwaged, it is often monotonous and demanding. But it is crucial to the whole capitalist enterprise. In the end the arguments all point again in the direction of the domination of capital over the lives of people. Men and women are together slaves of the profit motive, yet they do not all share equally in the profits. In the end women are being *used.* They are seen as a commodity, they are dehumanized, in order to keep the capitalist wheels turning.

A Marxist feminist explanation of women's inequality is thus a much more full-bodied one than that of the liberal writers. For them the need is to look further than the individual to the structures of society, to historical processes, to the economic system. Different Marxist feminists have different emphases, different concerns and often different conclusions from each other, yet for all of them the commitment is 'to ask feminist questions, but to give Marxist answers'.

Two basic questions
There are two basic issues for us. Has Marxist feminism discovered the key to women's oppression, and can it now provide us with the tools to demolish the prison, and build something better in its place?

In tackling the first issue there is much in the Marxist account to which we would have to assent. The capitalist system has harshly exploited vulnerable workers, especially women workers in low paid jobs. The family has been changed to suit the system, so that woman-as-producer has become woman-as-dependent carrying out unwaged tasks to service the workforce. The profit motive has led to the degrading of women, in advertising, in pornography; it has manipulated people's wants against their best interests to keep the tills rattling. In all these ways the structures and motives of capitalism have affected the lives and the relationships of women.

Nevertheless, for all its insights there are some fundamental weaknesses with this analysis which we need to explore.

The most central criticism is that the Marxist account is at root *reductionist.* We saw in part one that the inequality-oppression of women takes a large number of forms, and occurs within a variety of institutions. There are very many aspects to it: physical, biological, psychological, historical, linguistic, social, economic, legal, aesthetic, familial, ecclesiastical. Human society is complex. What is more, the kinds of oppression are likely to be different in these different areas: what a woman experiences as frustration in a church service will be different from physical cruelty, derogatory sexist comments from judges, lack of promotion opportunities at work, or being housebound with small children. So to focus on one of these aspects, the economic, in order to explain the complexity of the whole is to leave questions unanswered. For although one would have to acknowledge that a capitalist economic structure has *implications* for all other aspects of society, *it does not explain them.* We cannot reduce legal, psychological, linguistic, etc. explanations to socio-economic ones.

The importance of this objection can be illustrated in a more specific problem: namely in the Marxist understanding of the family. Here reductionism is clearly evident. Most of us now would want to concede that a careful historical examination of early industrialization does show the effect of capitalism on the reorganization of the family yet it by no means logically follows that therefore the family *is only* an economically-constructed human arrangement. Even frequent references to polygamous societies will not make this point.

In fact such references muddle the feminist case, since under most polygamous cultures, especially of course polygynous ones with their extensive male ownership ethos, women actually experience less 'freedom' than under capitalism. Islamic societies, for example, are not known for their liberated women. All we can conclude from these examples is that the family takes a variety of social forms, and among the cultural variables which influence these is the system of production. But though this might explain the organization, it does not tell us anything about the *meaning of the family.*

Here I would want to suggest that the family as an institution cannot be reduced to being merely a pawn of the system. The family has its own identity and integrity. It is a complex set of relationships and the meaning of the family lies in the complex quality of those relationships. This is of course not to say that there are not economic aspects to family life. But it is to say that it cannot simply be *defined* in economic terms. Far from being merely an economic pawn the family has its own responsibility. It exercises economic choices: what to save, how to spend, whether to give, how to organize division of labour in the family and so on. Many of the choices of course are limited, and it is in understanding the limitations that a Marxist account has much to offer. Yet even within the same class or even the same wage group there is a great variety of family stewardships, which indicates that families do not experience life only within an economically-controlled system. Different beliefs and values held by families play an enormous part in influencing what the family looks like. Family relationships themselves then have a different reference point — one beyond and outside economics.

This does not mean we can feel complacent about the contemporary 'nuclear' form of the family. There is much wrong with it. But what is wrong with the family is not necessarily dictated by the structure of the economy: it is more likely to be a problem with the structure of relationships.

In some of their deepest experiences a Marxist analysis thus has nothing to say to women. An experience of deep joy, trust, contentment and peace within marriage will not be easily explicable to them in terms of the systems of production and reproduction. Nor will they recognize it as false consciousness—of having been duped by the ideology of romantic love which keeps them in bondage to the capitalist system. They know it to be something other: part of the *meaning of marriage* itself which in the end is not reducible.

It will be evident now that my argument is that a Marxist account does not in the end offer an adequate explanation for women's inequality. It does highlight some vital factors which have contributed to it, but its explanation of these can only be partial. How does it fare on the second count? Does it give us the way ahead: to reconstitute an oppression-free future?

Here I have to confess to being very pessimistic on two accounts.

First, it would be dispiriting for many women who are suffering now to learn that in the end only a massive economic and political reconstruction of society can alleviate their distress. For although Marxist feminists are active often alongside liberal feminists in their campaigns for legal reform, the fundamental belief is that without socialism there can be no *real* solution to women's inequality. Yet this faith itself brings another problem. For where Marxism has become the 'official religion' of a state we still have not seen the ending of oppression. It is true of course that what we may be witnessing is not true Marxism at all, but it is all the majority of women have to go on.

My second worry is a deeper one. The other half of the Marxist belief in the corruption of the capitalist system is faith in the working class. At the last stop they are still working from the Enlightenment perspective of the inherent ability of men and women to solve their own problems. The deep-down commitment is still to the inherent goodness of the human being and this makes the position an over-optimistic one in the end. Real sin, real greed, real corruption, real selfishness is at the centre of the human heart. A change in the system of production and allocation might resolve many issues, but it will not touch this one.

Notes

1. R. Owen, *A New View of Society* (Pelican 1970), p. 140.
2. J. Weeks, *Sex, Politics and Society* (Longman 1981), p. 169.
3. ibid., p. 170.
4. Juliet Mitchell, *Woman's Estate* (Penguin 1976), p. 95.

5. Sheila Rowbotham, *Woman's Consciousness, Man's World* (Penguin 1974), p. 58.
6. ibid., p. 59.
7. Juliet Mitchell, *Woman's Estate,* p. 108.
8. ibid., p. 107.
9. ibid., p. 181.
10. Felicity Edholm, 'The Unnatural Family' in E. Whitelegg (ed.) *et al., The Changing Experience of Women* (Oxford, Martin Robertson, 1982), p. 177.

9:   Radical Feminism

Radical feminists are the ones everyone thinks they know about. They are labelled the aggressive women, the ones always inciting other women to belligerence, the ones undermining the position of any woman who chooses to be 'just a housewife'. They are the ones who are against everything, the ones never content with any legal reform, the slogan-makers, the man-haters. As far as many Christians are concerned they oppose all that is good and decent in society.

Yet radical feminism is easier to stereotype than to define. Nor can one always point to an identifiable group and say, there are the *radicals*. In Britain at least, radical feminists are as likely to be found dispersed among other groups as in their own closely-knit alternative communes. What is more there are degrees of radicalism. Some who call themselves radical feminists will do so because they *feel* radical about their feminism and see it as the central aspect of their lives. Others call themselves radical because they oppose the norm of heterosexuality: they maintain the right to be open about sexual preferences. Others are radical because they espouse a totally woman-centred ideology which can be played through in every aspect of life. Others are radical because they have rejected both the liberal and Marxist analysis of the causes of inequality, and insist on a more fundamental diagnosis. There are also differences in political involvement. Many radical feminists are closely identified with politics of the left, maintaining with Robin Morgan that 'Women are the real Left'[1]: what is needed therefore are policies which are more *radically* left than anything envisaged before. Others, however, maintain that their woman-centred analysis has no counterpart at all in conventional politics, and that their position is essentially an apolitical one. Finally, there are stages of development. The biological determinism of the early 1970s gave way to a much fuller preoccupation with patriarchy and culture.

What we see, then, is a very complex and involved picture when we turn to radical feminism. Certainly, radical feminists are women who are angry, but their anger has many different levels. Rather than explore all of these, this chapter aims to look more at the root cause of their anger and in doing so to open up their own distinctive analysis of the problem of inequality.

The rise of radical feminism has been well documented. It grew out of the civil rights movement and the New Left, and the liberal feminist activity at the end of the 1960s. It began to some extent like the American women's suffrage movement some 130 years earlier out of a concern for those who were black and oppressed, and ended by identifying and focusing on another oppressed group—women themselves. Because of this it is difficult to point to writers in the past and claim they form the basis for contemporary radical feminism. In so many ways it was a new departure. It belongs uniquely to the late twentieth century. Yet in another sense it was not new. Writers from Mary Wollstonecraft onwards have had radical traits in their analyses of the situation of women: traits which indicated that more was necessary than legal reforms, better education or even a change of the economic system. Even though it has now utterly departed from the individualism of the Enlightenment, radical feminism is still a post-Enlightenment phenomenon. In ways which we shall explore later it takes its cue from the Enlightenment perspective on human personhood.

This chapter, however, will be focusing on less than twenty years of radical feminist history—from its beginnings before 1970 to the present day. For these years alone have yielded so many changes and variations, so much scholarship and writing that they are a rich field for the student of feminism to harvest. As well as demonstrating the shifts in feminist thinking and analysis, they also show us the key areas of radical feminist concern, and we shall pluck these carefully one by one to examine, evaluate and maybe taste for ourselves.

The need for a new movement

For some, the 1960s was a period of much heart-searching. The affluent society had not brought contentment. It seemed to some that those in authority had little concern for justice and equality, and the frequent invoking of the American Constitution was little more than a mockery. The whole Vietnam episode was seen by many of its critics to be simply a case of America meddling in an often bloodthirsty way in the internal affairs of another country. The alleged imperialism of the US, along with what they perceived to be blatant hypocrisy over gross inequalities, racism and the growth of a police state encouraged students and others, on both sides of the Atlantic, to engender their own activity, hostile to authority. It was more than mere 'student unrest'. In some cases it amounted to a full-blown agenda for tackling the problems at source; new concepts crept into the language; new methods were developed; sit-ins, marches, demonstrations, occupations became a visible feature of this organized outcry. Awareness, Brotherhood and Power were woven as strands into the very clothing they wore.

However, these very same methods were soon to be used by another group, and against the men who had introduced them into the language of conflict. For it soon became evident that the vision of equality, the dream of an oppression-free society did not extend to include women. The women activists increasingly became conscious that they were not included in any of the decision-making processes but were instead saddled with domestic and ancillary chores. What was worse, when the women raised this as an important issue they were met with contempt, humiliation and ridicule. Quite why this should have been the case is not easy to understand. Certainly, the attitude was reminiscent of those earlier Marxists who did not want to trivialize their case with that of women's rights. It is also true that in the New Left at that time was a hard and tough 'macho' emphasis. However, for whatever reason, the damage was done and women soon recognized that in order to effect any change in their own situation a new movement was needed: a *women's* liberation movement.

The techniques of the Left thus became part of the new movement of radical women. Demonstrations and marches replaced political and legal lobbying. The demonstrations against national 'beauty' competitions, which, they argued, devalued women and paraded them as sex objects became a well-publicized feature. Consciousness-raising became the tool whereby women could experience together the extent of their mistreatment and suffering. False consciousness was to be stripped away, and through communal sharing and relating common frustrations the real situation could be exposed.

Sisterhood became the means by which such women could then be supported and nourished. Womanpower was a reality. Summing up the new hope was the title of Robin Morgan's book *Sisterhood is Powerful* (1970). So a new language had replaced the language of liberal, 'equal rights' feminism. 'Inequality' had become 'oppression', 'emancipation' had been superseded by 'liberation'. The new movement had departed significantly from the liberal women's movement and from the male Marxist movement. Women had indeed become the real New Left.

Male exclusion

It would be difficult to underestimate the effect of that scorn and contempt given to women who were active in the American left-wing groups. The rift between radical men and radical women in the US was to be permanent and on a level which has never been experienced to quite the same extent in Britain. It also highlighted the nature of the root problem itself. For if the men who were closest to them ideologically and communally exhibited such deep-seated hostility and hatred when challenged, then what did this say about the men who were out of view? Strong anti-male attitudes were therefore evident from the start in radical feminism. They varied from excluding men from meetings, to writing up a manifesto for SCUM: the Society for Cutting Up Men. One large American feminist organization would only allow a small quota of their members to be in any permanent or semi-permanent relationship with a man.

Yet there are more important reasons than reaction to the hostility of the male New Left which have produced this negative attitude to men. The first is the deep-seated belief that most men devalue women and see them in terms of self-gratification. Since interest in a woman's arguments moves so quickly to interest in a woman's body, meetings which included men were quite likely to have this hidden agenda which would keep women in the very roles they were fleeing from. A still more serious allegation, made by a large number of articulate radical feminists, is that most men actually hate women. This was certainly the belief behind the manifesto of SCUM. Germaine Greer, too, who has reached a large number of women in Britain particularly, echoed these sentiments in *The Female Eunuch* (1971). She began a chapter entitled

'Loathing and Disgust' with the observation: 'Women have very little idea of how much men hate them'. This hatred, encouraged and fostered during adolescence, is related to biology and sex, where it manifests itself in an ugly and often degrading way. Once a man has satisfied himself sexually his loathing becomes clear: 'I wanted to strangle her right there in my bed then go to sleep.' Women are seen not as persons but only in terms of the functions they perform: '. . . the only interesting women are the available ones: they do not think more highly of the unavailable girls for they find in such exclusivity only the desire to strike a harder bargain: these are the bitches, the others are the slags.' Rape too now has another definition. It is not simply the product of uncontrollable sexual attraction, nor is it seen in terms of economic manipulation and exploitation. It is nothing other than an expression of woman-hatred: 'The act is one of murderous aggression, spawned in self-loathing and enacted upon the hated other. Men do not themselves know the depth of their hatred.'[2] A few do know however, and they are given special attention in *The Female Eunuch.* In a brilliant style, characteristic of the feminist writers of the early 1970s Germaine Greer whipped her words into stinging indictments of the self-devaluation which women are taught to experience, because of the loathing of men. Small wonder, therefore, that crucial to the new awareness of women was that men should be excluded from their gatherings.

Another reason for male exclusion was much more pragmatic. Since men are used to having authority and leadership, whenever they are present in a group they will simply take it over. Work by Dale Spender, and many others since, has produced convincing evidence that despite beliefs to the contrary, men in mixed groups talk far more than women.[3] Men are used to 'handling' issues, whether intellectual, business, financial, organizational. Men are used to being listened to. They are not used to sharing leadership or decision-making with women. This was evidenced from the beginning of radical feminism when male sympathizers assumed leadership of the groups they belonged to, thus reinforcing the very issue in question: that of male dominance.

A new diagnosis
The crucial issue which this leads us to is that the radical

feminists had moved into a new diagnosis of the reasons for inequality. Inequality, as we have seen, was no longer just about lack of personal rights or privileges. Nor was it about unfair allocation of resources. Inequality was now subsumed under the bigger concept of oppression: in that, the Marxists were right. And oppression was not about specific individual actions, but about structures: economic, biological, social and familial. The Marxists were right there too. What is more, it was true that there were two classes: the oppressors and the oppressed; those in power, those exploited. But the dividing line was no longer the ownership of the means of production. The big divide was not now between capitalist and worker. The dividing line was sex, and the two classes were men and women. Men, as a *sexual class,* were the oppressors. Women, as a *sexual class,* were the oppressed. Marxism in the end offered the wrong analysis of women's subordination, and the wrong solution. Waiting for a massive change of the economic and political system was anyway rather like pie in the sky for women oppressed now. But for some radical feminists this idea of a socialist utopia was itself utterly irrelevant. It would merely replace one set of men with another, and from their own experience, Marxist men were equally as sexist as capitalist men. Sex is a form of oppression independent of social class.

The root problem was therefore not with the social class dominance of the *economic* system; it was with the male dominance of the *patriarchal* system. Liberal feminism had accepted patriarchy without any significant challenge, because patriarchy formed the very underpinnings of liberalism. Marxist feminism did recognize patriarchy, but saw it as secondary to the class struggle. In the end, when capitalism is removed, along with it will go the very foundations of patriarchy. The memory of a patriarchal system might of course remain for some time later and still affect the relations between men and women, but the crippling blow will have been dealt. The radical feminists, however, were not happy with that. Patriarchy, the legitimized and institutionalized domination of men over women, was the very problem itself. How could it be some derivative of capitalism, when men have dominated women throughout history?

Yet even though they reject the Marxist diagnosis it is evident how heavily some radical feminists lean on its analysis. As Olive Banks points out: 'radical feminist writers often treat men as an exploiting class as if they were completely analogous to the ruling class of Marxist orthodoxy, except that the class war becomes a war between the sexes.'[4] Kate Millett in particular is singled out in this respect as simply replacing 'class' with 'sex'. In a passage in *Sexual Politics* (1971) she gives a formulation of patriarchy which could easily be transposed as a Marxist formulation of the ruling class within capitalism. '[This] society . . . is a patriarchy. The fact is evident at once if one recalls that the military, industry, technology, universities, science, political office and finance—in short, every avenue of power within the society, including the coercive force of the police, is entirely in male hands.'[5]

Patriarchy, then, is the enemy. Patriarchy exists everywhere; it is the 'prevailing religion of the entire planet'.[6] Women live in a male-controlled world, and this control is exercised not merely on the fringes of their experience, but in the very act of identifying themselves as women. Women have to define who they are through male eyes and have to win male approval or *pay the price.* Patriarchy is the power structure at work, in the home, at school, in the Church and in the government. Some will raise their eyebrows in disbelief and point to women prime ministers, headteachers, administrators or managing directors, but the radical feminists are not convinced. The mere *presence* of women in decision-making capacities does not challenge patriarchy, because the vast majority of these women are themselves upholding and reinforcing patriarchy by the kinds of decisions they make. The system is bigger than any individual. Indeed any individual woman opposed to patriarchy is unlikely ever to be in a position to make her opposition felt. She will have had to play the male game to achieve any status in the first place. Only through the women's movement can an effective coherent attack be mounted, and when it is, the scorn and backlash of the patriarchal culture—of women and men—will be vitriolic.

We can see that the patriarchal explanation of inequality is more all-embracing than even the Marxist one. Take the division of public and private, for example. Radical feminists do not only expose this division, they bring their analysis into the very domain of the private. *The personal is political* has become a key phase. The politics of patriarchy do not stop at the front door. They come right into the home. They are present in the very bedroom. This is why nothing escapes the scrutiny of radical feminism. Sex itself is as much a part of its investigation as is the world of work. The politics of orgasm are as important as the politics of capitalism. For the *male-as-norm* in society is what is under attack. Instead, what is significant for women is significant for social analysis. No area can any longer be seen as 'neutral'. It is all male-centred. Patriarchy dominates everything.

Fifteen years of feminist writing has hardened attitudes towards many former allies. In Britain, the bonding between Marxist and radical feminism has remained strong, with an interesting dual course being steered by many. But in the US there has been increasing disenchantment and weariness with the Marxist stance. By 1979 Mary Daly was dismissing Marxism and Maoism along with Christianity and Islam as all subscribing to patriarchy. By 1980 Adrienne Rich had summarized the disillusioned impatience of contemporary radical feminists with the old ideas of the 1960s:

For many of us, the word 'revolution' itself has become not only a dead relic of Leftism, but a key to the deadendedness of male politics: the 'revolution' of a wheel which returns in the end to the same place; the 'revolving door' of a politics which has 'liberated' women only to use them, and only within the limits of male tolerance.'[7]

So within the radical camp itself there have been developments. But having identified patriarchy as the fundamental problem questions still remain. How was it brought about, and how is it reinforced? If it is not simply upheld by the exclusion of women from public life, or by woman's complex relationship to the two worlds of production and reproduction, what underlies patriarchy to make it so effective? In the sections that follow I am going to focus on two different kinds of answers which they give: one to be found in biology, the other to be found in culture.

Biology is destiny
One response is to be found in the work of Shulamith Firestone and Susan Brownmillar. Although they come to different conclusions each of them takes biology and human

anatomy as her focal point, and finds in the biological differences between man and woman the clue to women's oppression.

In *The Dialectic of Sex* Shulamith Firestone seizes upon *childbearing* as the central point of women's oppression. The cause of exploitation is found in the biological differences between men and women. Anatomy is indeed destiny. Bearing children, menstruating, lactating and undergoing menopause all mark women off from men and ensure their oppression. Women will never achieve freedom until they are freed from these functions.

Her book then lashes out at pregnancy, motherhood, the 'biological family', the ideology of love and the dependence of women and children. Her attack is devastating: 'Pregnancy is barbaric . . . [It] is the temporary deformation of the body of the individual for the sake of the species.'[8] But we accept pregnancy as part of motherhood and the biological family. Yet these institutions themselves cripple and exploit women. The family is 'the vinculum through which the psychology of power can always be smuggled'. Whilst the family exists 'the tapeworm of exploitation can never be annihilated'. Why are women so slow to recognize this? It is because of the myth of love. This 'love' is in fact 'the pivot of woman's oppression', yet it is not real love, the love which she herself envisages in her dependence-free utopia. It is a smokescreen, a romantic ideology. It is the mask which disguises the power relationships that operate in marriage and creates the myth of equality. It justifies keeping women in dependence. Women's lives are thus structured in such a way which keeps them in perpetual bondage. But in the end this is because of biological differences.

Her proposed programme of reform was an extremely ambitious one. Its aim was 'the freeing of women from the tyranny of reproduction by every means possible, and the diffusion of childrearing to the society as a whole.'[9] Childbearing was to be taken over by technology; artificial reproduction could remove the task from women. It would even be feasible to insert a human embryo into the uterus of a cow where the gestation period could be accomplished without burden to the mother. Once born, children would belong to a household of, say, ten or so 'contracting-in' adults who would share the child-care arrangements. Thus the present pattern of 'psychologically destructive genetic parenthood' would be replaced and instead 'all relationships would be based on love alone, uncorrupted by dependencies and resulting class inequalities'.

Shulamith Firestone was probably the first, but not the last, of the radical feminists to urge artifical reproduction as a means of freeing women. Others since have advocated the splitting of the ovum to produce female offspring as part of their programme for liberation. There is one difference, however. For some of these later feminists the motive is to rid themselves of any dependency on men, even for the next generation. It is seen as a possible part of a woman-centred ideology. Even then, it is not a popular position. But for Shulamith Firestone artificial reproduction was the way out of the biological system which in itself limited the extent of woman's freedom. As long as women were slaves to their anatomy, men would take advantage of the 'natural reproductive' difference between them. A unisex society was the new utopia: one which eliminated the biological difference between the sexes.

There are obviously many problems with this position, and it has not been accepted by many feminists in the 1980s. To start with it is not clear to what extent these differences in biology *produce* social and psychological structures. Secondly, the concept of love is difficult to grasp. Love based on blood ties or motherhood is seen as unreal love, as only an ideological whitewashing. Real love is instead the free act of free, unrelated individuals, but seems to involve little commitment of any kind. Adults contracting in and out of households, children transferring out if they wish, and everyone enjoying sex without homosexual, paedophilic or incest taboos seems a strange basis for enduring and loving relationships. Other problems centre on the extremity and naivety of the envisaged reforms. The big question remains 'Who will be in control?' Who will establish the 'contracting rules' for the households? Who will be in charge of the artificial reproduction programme? The assumption that it will be women seems to be ungrounded. Will the eradication of biological differences, even if it were possible, go anywhere towards an equal society, or are the factors of male domination deeper than biology?

Shulamith Firestone's position is one of *biological determinism.* Women's oppression is somehow programmed into the very cells of her structure. The only way out for women is thus one of radical reconstruction. But most of us would feel very uneasy about a programme involving genetic engineering or artificial reproduction. So should she. For if men are powerful and evil enough to exploit women because they bear children, how will it change when they have the future of the human race at the bottom of a test tube?

In *Against our Will: Men, Women and Rape,* Susan Brownmillar presents us with an alternative biological hypothesis to the origins of patriarchy. She argues that the possibility of rape bestows and perpetuates male domination over women. Because human beings, unlike other animals, do not mate in season, the sex act is not dependent on the female's receptivity. So men can insist on intercourse when it suits them, and because of her usual muscular weakness a woman is in no position to resist. In fact the male anatomy gives man the 'structural capacity' to force intercourse on a woman against her will. In a highly speculative passage Susan Brownmillar outlines a brief history of rape, suggesting that the first act of rape was probably an accident, but from then on the human male recognized he had a weapon by which women could be conquered. Since then rape has become 'nothing more or less than a conscious process of intimidation by which *all men* keep *all women* in a state of fear.'[10]

One of the important features of this account was a redefinition of the rapist as non-deviant. The rapist is an ordinary 'normal' man, and rape for a man is a 'normal' biological act, albeit a violent and woman-hating one. All men are potential rapists; all women are potential victims. However, Susan Brownmillar's programme for change breaks out of a determinist pattern. For although the root of the problem is biology she is not advocating Shulamith Firestone's way forward. Nor does she seem to be advocating universal castration. Instead she argues that the women's movement can of itself make up the limitations of anatomy. It can teach women to defend themselves, individually and collectively, and thus break men's power over them. Defence need not always take a physical form. The support of rape crisis centres, the educating of the public about rape, and changes in legislation to make it a more serious crime would all contribute to the power-breaking pattern. In fact of course, unlike the earlier proposals, many of these have been adopted by the feminist movement at large, and many women with no previous contact with feminism have come to an affiliation with it through their own experiences of help at rape crisis centres.

Even though the end product is very different, Shulamith Firestone and Susan Brownmillar both construct an argument which again is fundamentally *reductionist.* The biological 'facts' provide the basic starting-point and are used in some sense to 'explain' the social, psychological and cultural structures built upon them. But other feminists reject this biological determinism, just as they rejected the economic determinism of Marxism. Men do dominate women, and this certainly involves sexual and biological domination. But without this domination biological differences on their own would be harmless enough. What needs to be dealt with therefore is not biology but the patriarchal *culture* which highlights and abuses the differences between the sexes.

Culture, not biology

It is an emphasis then on this 'culture' rather than 'nature' which has become the mainstream radical feminist preoccupation. It is patriarchal culture which takes differences of 'nature' and makes them into something far bigger. In order to change patriarchy then it is pointless to try to change biology; much more important is to work on the attitudes and ideas people hold.

A distinction then was drawn early on between *sex* and *gender.* Sex is the biological category: it refers to the division of male and female. Gender however is the social-cultural category. It refers to the expectations, attitudes and ideas which attach themselves to 'male' and 'female'. To be female is simply to have a certain anatomy. To be a woman is to be surrounded by a whole set of gender assumptions: ideas of femininity, appropriate roles and behaviour. The problem is that most people do not recognize the difference between sex and gender. They see all their attitudes about being a woman as part of the natural order of things. They are 'givens'. This then is what radical feminists are attacking. They are suggesting instead that the ideas we have of women and men are culturally conditioned and *socially constructed.*

A vitally important task then is to uncover these ideas and assumptions about the sexes: to examine what are these *gender stereotypes* in our society. What is it to be manly? Most people would have a set of ideas including some of the following: aggressive, dominant, brave, self-reliant, active, persistent, rational, and so on. Men are more scientific than women, and less emotional. 'Femininity', on the other hand is being passive, weak, flatterable, gullible, affectionate, sensitive, less rational but more caring than a man. These stereotypes, and many others, are not merely widely held, they form the basis for the way many of us live. They are used by advertisers to sell their products, by schools in organizing their timetables, by TV writers in scripting their characters, by clergymen in writing their sermons, by judges in giving sentence and by parliamentarians in passing laws. Most of us allow stereotypes to structure our own behaviour, rather than think our way through them, *yet they are often grossly inaccurate.*

Why do they persist? The feminists believe it is because they are part of the patriarchal culture; they are the way men justify their domination of women; they are the court of appeal for behaviour and laws which if applied to men themselves would be seen as blatantly unjust. Women have been denied many things on the grounds of these assumptions. They have been seen as too irrational to study law, too feeble to take on a 'man's job', too unreliable to be given the vote, and too emotional to have their finger on the button. At the same time rigid assumptions about what it is to be a nice girl, a clean housewife, a good mother, an efficient secretary have all reinforced their roles as subservient to men. The unfortunate thing is that women have fulfilled their role expectations all too well, and the predictions have become self-fulfilling. This is why women need to be liberated: they need to be free to decide for themselves what it is to be a woman, and not to have male attitudes thrust upon them.

This division between sex and gender means that we no longer need to accept the 'normal' as the 'natural'. An appeal to the 'natural' has always been a stock response of patriarchy. It is natural for a woman to do the housework. It is natural for a man to earn more. It is natural for boys to be mechanical, for girls to like dolls. But this 'natural' almost always has nothing to do with 'nature' or with biology. More often than not it is merely a statement of what is normal. Yet what is normal is to see things as a man sees them. To be normal is to be male. 'Why can't a woman be more like a man?'

So a challenge to the male norm has now come on several fronts. Science, social science, history and the arts have been displayed as predominantly male. Sociology and psychology have traditionally been full of male assumptions. What has been presented as neutral, objective data, especially on women, are studies done by men with very male-centred methodologies. If a husband helped once a week with some small household chore, it was entered as an example of shared domestic roles! History was always the history of men. Economics ignored the enormous part played by women in the domestic economy. The psychology of women was almost invariably written by men. Even studies on mother-hood and women's sexuality have been carried out by men and, as far as the feminists are concerned, with disastrous results. A new flurry of women writers, taking a woman-aware look at some of these topics, began to produce very different findings. Everything was tackled, from philosophy to female orgasm, and radical feminism moved into a new phase.

Woman-centred ideology

Yet it was not without precedent. As long ago as 1954 Simone de Beauvoir had identified this separation from man as woman's fundamental problem. She had referred to woman as always being the *Other.* The woman-centred ideology was now prepared to carry this through to its ultimate conclusion. Let woman be *Other.* Consciousness-raising had shown it was possible. Now was the time to bring a woman-centred analysis into every aspect of life. So Women's Studies Courses became features of university and college programmes, implicitly conceding that up to now all studies had been men's studies. The problem with patriarchy had been its very invisibility and its supposed neutrality. Now it was given clothes it could be identified. Now the assumed objectivity of male scholarship could be challenged. Feminist research over the last ten years has done precisely that, involving both Marxist and radical feminist perspectives. A few titles make their own point: *Science and Sexual Oppression* (1981), *Sex, Politics and Society* (1981), *Biological Politics* (1982), *Childhood and Sexuality* (1982), *Women and Their Doctors* (1978), *The Sociology of Housework* (1974), *Girls, Wives and Factory Lives* (1981), *Gender, Class and Work* (1983),

Doing Feminist Research (1981). Hundreds of articles and books have been produced.

However, there were other aspects to being Other which were not simply to present a systematic *theoretical* challenge to the patriarchal culture. It involved a critique of masculinity itself, and all that it stood for in society. Amongst radical feminists were those who wanted to foster and develop those very qualities which had been seen as specifically feminine: non-competitiveness, sensitiveness, imagination, sharing and nurturing. Motherhood was no longer despised as preventing women from being full persons, but mothering was now seen as being the very vehicle through which feminine qualities could be fostered. Yet it was mothering with a difference: mothering with its back to patriarchy. Being a mother in a woman-centred culture thus came into its own. In a similar vein, women's groups, long established on a non-leadership, sharing basis, found ways of drawing each member into discovering her particular gifts and expressing her identity in the unity of the group. Male ideas of 'excellence' were abandoned for feminine ideas of mutual creativity. Editorship, and production teams of journals and newsletters would rotate, for example, so that each woman might learn skills in a supportive community. An alternative to patriarchy had thus been established, both in science and scholarship, in community and domestic life. It drew upon and was nourished by the enriching qualities which women in a state of freedom could abundantly express.

Some readers will begin to feel confused at this point. Surely there is a kind of double-take here? If we have abandoned the 'natural' and the stereotypes of manliness and feminity, then where do we get these particularly womanlike qualities from? We cannot both dismiss gentleness, sensitivity and warmth as just socially-constructed stereotypes when attacking patriarchy, but recall them when wanting to construct a woman-centred alternative. This is an issue to which we shall return later.

Goddess worship

There are two other aspects to a woman-centred ideology which we have not examined. One is a new interest in worship, in 'things of the soul'. One variety of this has found prominence in America. Mary Daly's new 'metaphysical feminism' effectively moves right outside any social implications of feminism at all. She sees all of feminist activity, whether liberal, Marxist or radical, from legal reform, rape crisis centres to Women's Studies as still taking place within patriarchy. Like the seditious material which Winston finds in *Nineteen Eighty-Four* the system knows all about, and will even encourage it, knowing at the end of the day that its control is total. There can be no escape therefore, except an escape *within*. At least in this account of patriarchy there seems to be no 'thought police'. Her feminism thus becomes other-worldly and very subjective. In many ways it is feminism at its most pessimistic.

Less so by far is the new interest in the 'soul' and 'supernatural' exhibited in the goddess cult. The argument is that for thousands of years before the rise of Judaism and Christianity and all the other 'male' religions, the universal deity, the life-force of the universe was the goddess. She was worshipped in a variety of ways, and for 'countless millennia' before men took control. What her modern followers are doing is simply to rediscover the power available in this celebration of ultimate femininity. 'It is the creation of a new life centred upon the adoration and celebration of the beautiful and vibrant creative force of the universe.'[11] Rites, priestesses, sacrifices become embedded in the experiences of those who follow these paths.

Nevertheless, at the same time as we can recognize that there are feminists who need to have this female goddess as vital to their total experience as women, it does not really follow that because a goddess was worshipped in ancient times we should worship one today. The sun and moon were also worshipped at various stages. So were War, Beauty, the Underworld, Thunder and the Sea. It would also seem that, for some, the desire is simply to have a god(dess) in their own image.

Radical lesbians

'Feminine spirituality' has affected only a small number of radical feminists. 'Coming out' and declaring themselves to be lesbian has affected many more. For lesbianism has been much more than preferring women sexually. It is seen also as a strong political statement. If the personal really is political then to decline heterosexual relationships is the mark of fully political, fully autonomous woman. To be a lesbian is thus the most personal and the most political stand a radical feminist can make. It is the final refusal.

Being a lesbian is therefore for many the logical outcome of a woman-centred ideology. Lesbianism draws together so many different strands. It attacks again the idea of the 'natural'. If a woman really can find deeper sexual fulfilment with another woman, how can anyone maintain the naturalness of heterosexual relations? It challenges again the dependence of women on men. It flouts the patriarchal structure of family and marriage. It turns its back on masculinity where it will hurt the most. The message is clear: men are irrelevant. Patriarchy does not have the last word. An alternative woman-centred culture is workable in every way.

But lesbianism is not merely a defiance towards male domination, the 'rage of all women condensed to the point of explosion'.[12] It is also a belief that only women can give to each other a real sense of self, of personal identity. It is seen by those involved as a process of healing, of emotional growth and tenderness which is impossible within heterosexual relations. Put simply, heterosexuality means 'men first'. Through this recovery of personal worth and growth, a woman is now better able to reach out to others. She is better able, too, to be a mother.

The need to mother is actually held as important in some lesbian relationships. In fact this need is usually denied. Not only is it still unlikely that a practising lesbian will ever be allowed to conceive through AID, it is unlikely that she will be allowed custody of any children from a previous marriage. So it does raise a question mark over the autonomy of radical lesbianism. Male critics have been quick to point out that women cannot be independent of men to this final extent. For a woman to *be* a mother a man is needed. How can the radical lesbian remain woman-centred if she will accept male sperm, even from a man who might make no claims as a father? The problem is a great one, and for some leads right back to artificial reproduction and the splitting of the ovum. The full extent of the difference between Shulamith Firestone's programme and the needs of a woman-centred approach can now be seen. Yet these alternatives to 'biological reproduction' remain still only hypothetical. They might 'solve' the problem in theory, but this is not the situation which lesbians live with now. At a deep level it has to lead to a compromise in the radical lesbian position.

The central issues for lesbians do not revolve around their ability to have and raise children, however. More important is to learn to know and love each other, and through that to know and love themselves. What they seek is not to persuade all radical feminists to be lesbian, but to be received and fully endorsed by their heterosexual sisters. Many have been deeply hurt by men and need a new basis for accepting themselves. Together they have to disengage from 'male-defined responses' and build up a full consciousness of being woman.

Radical feminism assessed

Attempting an overall appraisal of radical feminism is not an easy thing to do. To start with, it seems such an *academic* task. But we are not simply looking at a collection of theories or ideas. The political is also personal, and the personal lives and experiences of many women are bound up in a deep and committed way to feminism. Another issue is of course that any argument I raise will already have been accepted by some radical feminist herself, who will have worked out some response to it in her own life.

However, it is still necessary to look again at the *main* position which radical feminists adopt, because this is both its biggest strength and weakness. The idea of patriarchy is too all-embracing: it has become a total explanation which bodes no exception and which involves the same kind of inevitability as a crude Marxism might have. It also offers no room for differences within patriarchy. As some Marxists point out, sisterhood has no meaning when it is used to link together a black, unemployed cleaner with five children to keep, and the daughter of a shipping tycoon at finishing school in Switzerland. Differences in class, race and colour play an important part in deciding social differences. Woman's oppression has so many levels that to ascribe it all to this universal phenomenon of 'patriarchy' cannot produce a fine enough analysis. What is also true is that it cannot help us to understand *men's* oppression, either, in the kind of detail we would like. Both the Marxists and radicals would recognize that some men also suffer oppression under the class and patriarchal systems. But if patriarchy exists for men, why should they? Certainly some of the stereotypes of masculinity force men to act roles which they can play only inadequately but this surely indicates that there is something wrong with the centrality of the idea of male domination. It no longer seems as if all males are involved.

Another similar set of problems follows. For, if a patriarchal culture is one where some men are also oppressed, it would seem that some women are not. How can we account for this? It could be of course that these women are in a state of false consciousness: they have been taken in by the system, and do not recognize how subjugated they are. I am sure that in fact there are many women of whom this would be true. But what of the others? Could it be that they do not experience oppression because *they are not oppressed?* In meeting and talking to a large number of women over many years, I am also sure that there are many who are in this category, which suggests that the all-embracing concept of 'patriarchy' needs to be refined a little.

One way of doing this is to draw distinctions within patriarchy. Most of what is attacked by radical feminists could be described as 'malignant patriarchy'—the ideology where men dominate women, intend to dominate women, and see it as natural that they should dominate women. Yet there are much more 'benign' forms of patriarchy where male presence (and even male leadership) does not entail male domination. In many areas of family life this benign patriarchy is at work: traditional roles are maintained, with the man as the main breadwinner and the woman assuming a larger share of domestic duties. Yet because both husband and wife are sensitive to each other's needs, and because this arrangement satisfies them both it would seem odd to talk about the woman being oppressed. So, although the situation would still be undeniably patriarchal, both internally and in relation to the wider culture, within the family itself it has assumed a 'benign' form. This would suggest that there is more to women's oppression than this big patriarchal system, and that society at large is composed of a whole range of institutions which might operate on non-oppressive lines. There are important implications of this for the whole radical feminist analysis. Oppression does not simply exist in a vacuum: it takes social forms all of which need explaining. To call it all 'patriarchal' means problems within specific institutions cannot always be dealt with in the right way. If a husband dominates a wife it is because there is something wrong with him and with the marriage. He is the one who needs to change first—not just the system.

One final problem which I promised we would return to is on the question of 'feminine qualities'. For here the source of these qualities is vital, since they are pivotal in the construction of the new society. Here the fundamental *longing* of radical feminism is so evident. Crucial to a woman-centred utopia must be love. Self-giving, sharing and caring, patience and joy are the very building blocks of the new future. Without these qualities there can be no utopia, no real way out of the mess which a man-centred society offers us. Therefore because these qualities cannot be derived from patriarchy they must somehow have their origin in woman herself. There can be no other source. The striking thing for Christians is how much these qualities sound like the biblical picture of the fruits of the Spirit: love, joy, peace, patience, kindness, goodness, faithfulness, gentleness, self-control. The difference is that in the biblical account these are not qualities which women have in themselves, *as women:* they are the fruits of living in the Spirit of God, the very Source of Love. What is more they are prescribed for men also. Within the Christian belief-system they make sense. They are an implicit part of the Good News. But radical feminism can provide no basis for these qualities. If gender characteristics are all socially constructed, how can any such qualities be inherent in womanhood?

Radical feminism wants the fruits then, but denies the Source. For in the end the stance of independence is independence from God also and an assertion of human (feminine) autonomy. Many of their diagnoses are correct. Much of what they have to say about patriarchy needs to be listened to. But at the deepest level is this problem. Their stance is a fundamentally religious one, and their faith is in themselves.

Notes

1. R. Morgan, *Going Too Far: The Personal Choice of a Feminist* (Random House, 1977), p. 130.

2. G. Greer, *The Female Eunuch* (New York, Bantam, 1972), pp. 249—51.
3. D. Spender, *Man-Made Language*. Routledge and Kegan Paul 1980.
4. O. Banks, *Faces of Feminism* (Oxford, Martin Robertson, 1981), p. 228.
5. K. Millet, *Sexual Politics* (Avon Books 1971), p.25.
6. M. Daly, *Gyn/Ecology: The Metaethics of Radical Feminism* (Boston, Beacon, 1978), p. 39.
7. A. Rich, *On Lies, Secrets and Silence: Selected Prose 1966—1978* (New York, W. W. Norton, 1979), p. 248.
8. S. Firestone, *The Dialectic of Sex: The Case for Feminist Revolution* (Jonathan Cape 1971), p. 224.
9. ibid., pp. 223—4, 270—1.
10. S. Brownmillar, *Against Our Will: Men, Women and Rape* (New York, Simon and Schuster, 1975), pp. 14—15.
11. W. Collins *et al., Directory of Social Change* (Wildwood House 1978), p. 14.
12. Quoted in H. Eisenstein, *Contemporary Feminist Thought* (Unwin 1984), p. 51.

PART THREE
SOME CHRISTIAN RESPONSES

To write about Christian responses to feminism is of course beset with problems, for the word 'Christian' has such a variety of meanings in institutionalized Christianity. Many who offer what feminists would regard as Christian reactions may not necessarily have any personal commitment to the Christian faith.

I have narrowed my considerations therefore to those who would confess a faith in Jesus Christ and show some seriousness towards the scriptural revelation. This therefore would not exclude per se *any of the major denominations although there would be many in those denominations whose reference point would be different.*

Again, I have chosen to represent the two 'poles' of Christian reaction: those whose response to the women's movement is one of indignation, righteous or otherwise, and who deny any substance to their case. Most of this group would also view any change in traditional roles with suspicion and alarm. The opposite pole consists of Christian women who have found in feminism a sharpening of their own identity, and a new heightening of their spirituality. At the same time there are those also who are now redefining the focus of their faith and worship, and for whom a woman-centred religion has replaced belief in a 'male' God.

10: Polarization: Christianity against Feminism

On the whole Christians do not react as hysterically to feminism as they did a decade ago. As more people within the Church have recognized the truth in some of the feminist arguments there has been a softening of attitudes and a willingness to listen. Some Christian women have noticed that the description feminists give of gender stereotypes tallies surprisingly with their own experiences as women within the Church. Men too have admitted that these same stereotypes can force them into behaviour patterns with which they feel uncomfortable. One issue in particular has drawn together the most radical feminists and the most conservative Christians: that of pornography. Although feminists recognize that it is from a very different position (one which they would call 'repressive'), they have accepted the support of Christians on the campaign against pornography, and barriers a decade thick have begun to shake, just a little.

In addition to the situation I have just described, attitudes to feminism within Christian circles are frequently split along political lines. For an undoubted feature of Christianity in the 1980s is the growth of polarized political camps. Those groups which have shown more sympathy with the 'left' wing have also been ready to meet feminists more than half-way on a large number of issues. At the same time they have faced an attack from the conservative 'right' which usually accuses them of moving away from the authority of the Scriptures. They have, it is argued, become theological relativists. In some cases of course this will regrettably be true, and yet in many instances the attack is unwarranted. Certainly it has also been the case within the reformed and evangelical positions that new stances taken up have been scripturally-directed, rather than scripturally-defiant.

Right-wing attitudes within the Church, (although not seen as right-wing by their adherents but as politically neutral!) continue their challenge and attack of contemporary feminism in a strident, often aggressive manner. Probably, amongst Evangelical and reformed Christians in the United States and Britain, this would even remain the pervasive attitude. The majority of Christians would react with irritation to the very notion of woman's oppression. Most would not be able to imagine how feminists can even posit this suggestion. The whole idea is ludicrous. What are these women *on* about? Others would more decisively see the women's movement as distinctly evil, as bent on destroying the Christian fabric of society. Some Christian men undoubtedly react in exactly the male chauvinist way already predicted of them. Christian women too often go to great lengths to denounce 'women's lib' and assert their own total commitment to their families, as if the the two were automatically incompatible. In some circles the mere mention of 'women's rights' is enough to start adrenalin cascading. Feminism is bad news. In lecturing to many Christian groups I have observed this attitude first hand. In reading the literature from this position I understand why.

Stereotypes of feminism
Many books and articles written by Christian authors have something detrimental to say about the women's movement. The most vehement are probably American. In those, even a mild veneer of courtesy to feminists is uncomfortably absent. What is frighteningly similar about all these writings however is (unavoidable) evidence that they start from a position of ignorance. Caricatures and stereotypes of feminists are curtly offered; accusations are hurled and indictments are made. Many lament the loudness and arrogance of feminists in tones like the Niagara Falls. Yet it is my firm conviction that most of these authors *have never read* any of the feminist writers they criticize and have little understanding of what they are saying. All feminism is the same: radical or extremely radical. There is usually no attempt to examine any of the major differences of approach or analysis, and little effort invested in checking the most basic allegations. Considering the number of careful (and scholarly) feminist works now available, this dismissal-without-examination is discourteous indeed. It is made even worse by the fact that the books or articles including such comments are frequently tritely written, handling important issues with such superficiality

that they can only do a disservice to the Christian reading public. The tragedy is that this material is all that many Christians ever look into.

Feminists then, according to popular Christian myth, are out to dominate men, to prove that they can wear the pants. Their main interest is to prove their superiority, both at work and in the home. A few examples, chosen at random, will make the point. Consider this passage taken from a British magazine which circulates to thousands of Christian women. Feminism, we are told, is 'a grim competition between the sexes, with the woman of today desperately trying to prove that what a man can do she can do better.'[1] In another book[2] the same point is made graphically, although jocularly:

Yet they are clearly wrong. Most forms of feminism eschew competition, and *domination* has never been a feminist aim. Nevertheless, the theme is echoed again and again. An American book this time, *The Christian Couple* by Larry Christenson, tells us 'Considerable rhetoric in the feminist movement can be translated into the simple complaint "Why can't we be where the important things are happening?" ' and later 'The radical feminists . . . are seeking with all the power of the modern media to impose another role upon women. When the verbal smoke clears what you are left with is the idea that the only life worth living is a man's life'.[3] It is a pity that where many others would see cogent arguments this writer only saw 'considerable rhetoric' and 'verbal smoke'. If he had been more prepared to investigate the fire he might have realized he had got the idea wrong. Which feminist is he talking about? Radical feminists are not interested in living a man's life. The whole point is that they want to live an oppression-free *woman's* life. However their critics are disinclined to consider such details.

The same theme takes a new twist in the next allegations, where 'The Women's Lib Morality' is blamed for contributing to family breakdown. We read:

In the name of equal rights for women a whole new life-style is creeping into the family domain, one that is weakening the father's role in the home at the expense of the marriage and the family. Feminine dominated homes are on the increase at an alarming rate, compounding the tragedies of marrige and the home.[4]

Feminists are also blamed for the widespread neglect of children: presumably because of 'feminine dominated homes': 'The most tragic victims of the feminist movement are today's children . . . the way many women treat their children [is] nice to have around but of secondary importance to their careers.'[5] And again: 'It is all too easy to be subconsciously influenced by women's lib and the current feminist drive into thinking that this role [of wife and mother] is somehow second-rate and scarcely worth the time and energy it requires.'[6] And yet again: 'With their skilful propaganda . . . the women's liberationists have managed to make the housewife's role seem one of uninterrupted drudgery.'[7] But again a central feminist argument is that it is the low status, both economic and social, which is given in capitalist and patriarchal society to the role of homemaker and mother which downgrades it. They are in fact frequently challenging this belittlement of women's work in the home. What is more, only feminists have ever seriously done *studies* on housewives and housework to understand how women themselves arrange work and what it means to them. Nor do feminists advocate the neglect of children or see them as secondary. Instead they offer a serious critique of contemporary *ideas* of mothering and suggest alternative models. We might not endorse all these models, but we need to consider them first.

Apparently feminists are also naive in their ambitions: 'Another unfortunate by-product of feminism is the way in which a younger generation has gained the impression that they can simultaneously have a successful career and a happy marriage and children without losing out in any way.'[8] Yet much feminist literature is devoted to this very problem. Another allegation on this theme simply raises a smile: 'The feminist movement is a strident declaration that women cannot and will not manage the home and family by themselves.'[9] Well, perhaps half-right. But the assumptions beind this comment are more important than the allegation itself. For who says women *should* 'manage the home and family by themselves'? This underlies the feelings still popular in some Christian groupings that women alone have responsibilities for the care of the family and home. We shall return to this later.

Feminists are also accused of urging women to sexual freedom and promiscuity, although very few have ever advocated promiscuity as the way to liberation. They are caricatured as downgrading real 'womanliness'—gentleness, patience and so on—although as we have seen, the women-centred feminist position highlights and fosters these qualities.

In the end cool reflection will show us that feminism is to blame for just about every social evil. 'As a by-product of the women's movement women are increasingly afflicted by ills previously mostly suffered by men. Lung cancer, heart diseases, alcoholism, and a decline in life expectancy . . . Suicide rates are up and women are also involved in crime.'[10]

We are left then with an utterly depressing picture of feminists as power-crazy, selfish, domineering career women, leaving devastation, misery and neglect in their wake. The astonishing factor is that they have persuaded other women to join them. Or have they? 'Christian women need to rise up and unanimously declare that the radical feminist protestors represent only themselves.'[11] Before this uprising takes place, and too much is declared, perhaps the evidence should be examined more carefully.

Stereotypes of man—woman relationships
Large-scale inaccuracies on the level we have just documented mean that a large proportion of the Christian public does not

get a chance to discover for itself what feminists are really saying. They simply manipulate those who read this invective into reacting negatively and stereotypically to all feminist positions and arguments. They also rule out the possibility of any 'true' Christian woman from espousing any form of feminism herself. They reinforce gender stereotypes, idealize traditional roles, and carefully avoid any discussion of patriarchy. Indeed, with little adjustments, they present Christianity as patriarchal, and those who challenge this identification as disobedient or non-Christian. It comes as no surprise then to see the very masculine—feminine generalizations which feminists challenge, heralded as the Christian Truth about Women: 'What a real woman wants is a real man. What a real man wants is a real woman. It is masculinity that appeals to a woman. It is femininity that appeals to a man. The more womanly you are, the more manly your husband will be.'[12] If we need to know what this 'masculinity' or 'femininity' amounts to, we need look no further than the non-Christian stereotypes thrown up by secular (predominantly American) culture. Yet this is wiped with an attempted Christian gloss. Weakness, dependence and vulnerability—all apparent features of 'femininity' are a woman's *God*-given characteristics: 'A woman's vulnerability . . . does not stop at the physical level. It includes also vulnerability at the emotional, psychological and spiritual level. Here too, she needs a husband's authority and protection.' She is so in need of protection as to be apparently incapable of exercising initiative or authority anywhere. 'It is the husband, not the wife, who is primarily responsible for what goes on in the home, the community and the church. When he deserts this role, or when the wife usurps it, both the home and the community . . . suffer for it.' What role has a woman then? The answer is simple: to submit to authority. 'Upon man is laid the authority to rule . . . Submission to authority means that you put yourself wholly at the disposal of the person who is set over you.'[13] And there you have it: total control, over total dependence. In case the single woman may begin to feel relieved she is out of this package, this author is swift to remind her that even she has no independence, but must look for her authority to the male members of the Church.

Then there is this whole question of androgyny—the 'equality' and reversibility of gender roles. What about the

husband for example helping a little with the children —
changing nappies perhaps, feeding the toddlers? Our enquiries
are dealt with crisply: 'Foolish advice. Male physiology and
psychology aren't geared to it. A father's relationship with his
children can't be built mainly around child-caring experiences.' In fact it would be very dangerous to suggest
otherwise. 'This blurring of mother — father roles can have
harmful effects on children. Because many fathers now wash
dishes, bath the baby and perform other traditional female
tasks, their sons often don't know what it means to be a
man.' The suspicion one gets that this man does not like
housework is reinforced in another passage: 'A wife who
shifts her unpleasant household chores to her husband is
downgrading her own activities in her children's eyes.'[14]

Quite apart from the tortuous logic employed and references
made to male physiology and psychology, these passages are
packed with unexamined assumptions which are quite
unsupportable on biological, psychological or theological
grounds. They would never convince a woman with even the
mildest feminist leanings that they were not the pennings of a
male manipulator anxious, for his own benefit and self-
interest, to gain total domination over at least one woman
(his wife) and hopefully over a few more besides (the single
women in the Church). No doubt this author does exercise
his domination in a 'loving' way, yet women married to other
men might not be so fortunate, and might find themselves (as
many do) submitting to wife-battering, or sexual abuse.[15]

Women, then, are presented in certain fixed and stereotypic
terms. They are divided into the good and the bad. The good
ones are those who know their place, the ones who accept
leadership and male decisions without question. The bad
ones are the feminists. The totality of a woman's life and
roles, the variety of experiences she undergoes and tasks she
performs, the breadth of her insights and understanding on
so many issues are all shrunk into this narrow vision of what
it is to be a woman. The frightening thing is that this distorted
picture of Christian womanhood, and the unquestioned
'rightness' of traditional roles, has many women in its grip,
and prevents them from getting within a mile of growing into
maturity and knowing real freedom in Christ.

Notes

1. Sarah Warren, 'Femininity or Feminism' (*Christian Woman* November 1983), p. 16.
2. Roger F. Hurding, *Restoring the Image* (Paternoster Press 1980), p. 83. A useful book in other ways.
3. Larry Christenson, *The Christian Couple* (Kingsway Publications 1978), pp. 46, 141.
4. T. and B. La Haye, *Spirit Controlled Family* (Kingsway Publications 1980), p. 29.
5. 'Femininity or Feminism', p. 6.
6. Ann Warren, *Marriage in the Balance* (Kingsway Publications 1981), p. 44.
7. James Robinson, *Attack on the Family* (Tyndale House Publishers 1980), p. 36.
8. Ann Warren, *Today's Christian Woman* (Kingsway Publications 1984), p. 15.
9. *The Christian Couple*, p. 47.
10. Gloria Hope Hawley, *Frankly Feminine: God's Idea of Womanhood.* (Standard Publications 1981).
11. *Spirit Controlled Family*, p. 72.
12. Elizabeth Elliot, *Let Me Be a Woman* (Hodder and Stoughton 1979), p. 158.
13. Larry Christenson, *The Christian Family* (Kingsway Publications 1978), pp. 35, 37, 40.
14. ibid., pp. 44–5.
15. See E. Storkey, 'Wife Abuse', a survey in *Family*, April 1985.

11: Salvation through Feminism

The final step from Christian faith to apostasy is for some a very short one. It is short because so many previous steps have already been taken in that direction. Some who have by now taken that step will be encountered in this chapter. For here we are looking at the other 'pole' of Christian response to feminism. I have just documented the response which reiterates traditional roles and stereotypes and ignores the deeper social, political and economic questions which the women's movement is asking. Now we swing in the opposite direction and look at those Christians who have become so absorbed in feminist issues that they are in danger of losing their Christian distinctiveness altogether, of being engulfed by the most radical wing of the women's movement, and by a feminist theology which is by now unrecognizable to any in the Church.

It is clear from the outset, then, that we shall not be looking at the full range of Christian feminism. Instead we shall concentrate on only the last two of three identifiable groups. The first, and possibly smallest group, *biblical feminism,* will not concern us here. For they—we—would hold tenaciously to the authority of the Scriptures, although challenge many attitudes and ideas which people claim to have derived from them. The point of departure, however, is fundamentally different from that of the other two groups. For the second group, *broadly-Christian feminism,* would not see Scripture in this way. There would be those who reserve the right to 'select' from the biblical writings and tradition, and those who feel there is little left to select from. Disenchantment with sexism in the Church is echoed by disenchantment with sexism in the Scriptures, and there is not much to salvage from either. The final group, *post-Christian feminism,* includes those whose alienation from the Church has become complete. For them the entire Christian tradition is overwhelmingly sexist. The gospel is bad news, and there is no way of recovering any part of it for women.

Early theologians

The unease of the feminists with Christian tradition begins with the early Church Fathers. Tertullian, Chrysostom, Augustine and Aquinas are all viewed as misogynists. It is hard for them to forgive Tertullian for his heavy-handed treatment of women. 'You are the devil's gateway. How easily you destroyed man, the image of God. Because of the death which you brought upon us, even the Son of God had to die.'[1] Augustine similarly is said to argue that only *man* is made fully in the image of God, and again holds woman responsible for the Fall. To Chrysostom is imputed one of the earliest Christian justifications of the public—private dichotomy, and the forbidding of women ever to venture into the public arena. Aquinas' notion of woman as helpmeet is also seen as derogatory, since he accepts her as a helpmeet only in the process of procreation. In every other respect man is helped better by another man. Misogyny such as this was thus bound to influence the developing Church and ensured, as far as the feminists are concerned, that often pagan attitudes of the day became part of Christian practice. And although with the Reformation views of women improved considerably, they did not move far enough. Even Luther and Calvin still saw women as basically subservient to men. Barth's theology, they allege, continues the tradition.

Church history, and the history of Christian doctrine, is frequently an embarrassment to the contemporary Church. These allegations have certainly to be faced and recognized. At the same time, we need to make sure that what we take from these early writers is put in the context of all their works, and in the case of the Reformation writers, their practices also. Even though I am not as optimistic as William Oddie in *What Will Happen to God?* a fully contextual setting will certainly *soften* their misogyny. One point he makes in criticism of the feminists here remains vital, however. It is that in spite of the alleged woman-hatred, the Christian tradition (and, I would add, particularly since the Reformation) has granted women 'a more honoured position than that created for them in any other world religion, with the possible exception of Judaism'.[2]

No matter how embarrassing Christian tradition might be, however, it is not an area where we would want to argue vehemently. Some of us would even be prepared to concede that the Church has a lot to answer for. Nor would we necessarily feel that the other aspect of the quarrel with tradition, the attack on liturgy, is of fundamental significance. For as we have seen, Christian hymns and liturgy are full of male-orientated language. There is little doubt that work could be done to rewrite much liturgy in a way entirely in keeping with scriptural teaching, which would eliminate conscientiously a large portion of unacceptable sexism. Recognition that women are present, and need to be addressed personally, and not through the men in the congregation, would seem to me to be a central tenet of spiritual worship. We can even appreciate the plea: 'Only if we, women and men, are able to live in non-sexist Christian communities, to celebrate non-sexist Christian liturgies, and to think in non-sexist theological terms and imagery will we be able to formulate a genuine Christian feminist spirituality.'[3]

However, the problem arises as to where the revision stops. For eliminating references to brothers, men, soldiers, etc. is one thing, but rewriting sections of the Scripture which offend us by mentioning that God is Father or that Christ is male is moving away from disputes about liturgy and tradition on to disputes about doctrine, basic beliefs and commitment. With Christian and post-Christian feminism this is ultimately where the battle needs to be staged.

Is God the Father?
A fundamental problem for feminists within the Church is the maleness of the deity. For some it is the central and most crucial issue of their faith. Christ was a man, the Son of a Father. God, the Father, as Father must inevitably be seen as male. But if the very focus of our worship is male how can female personhood be significant? One tradition of course has postponed this problem by the elevation of Mary. As the mother of Christ Mary surely has a claim to be worshipped too? Thus she provides a point of identity for women in the Catholic tradition. However, Mary was only a woman. She was not God and most Catholics as well as Protestants would recognize this. So it must mean that divinity has to be identified with maleness and not femaleness. If this is so, then no wonder that women are oppressed. In this central tenet of the Christian faith we can see a legitimation of the whole system of patriarchal domination of women. What is

more, at the deepest level of their selfhood women are left with a God with whom they cannot identify and who cannot identify with them. For the disciplining, authoritarian figure of patriarchal Christianity is not one who knows what it is to be a woman, and where she hurts. Even the loving Christ can only see things from the vantage point of being a man. It is this most basic dilemma which Christian feminists face. How can woman be woman, and God be the Father? This problem has not escaped the notice of men in the Church. An American bishop, in an oft-quoted passage, has stated it well:

If God is male, not female, then men are intrinsically better than women. It follows then, that until the emphasis on maleness in the image of God is redressed the women of the world cannot be entirely liberated. For if God is thought of as simply and exclusively male, then the very cosmos seems sexist.[4]

Although the problem is easy to state, the solution is by no means so clear-cut for many feminists. The instinctive reaction is of course to say that the Church must have got it wrong. Because the Christian tradition was born into patriarchy, and itself reinforced patriarchy, the image of a patriarchal (male) God was all that was needed to complete the picture. But they argue God cannot simply be Father. One solution then is to move away from 'Fatherhood' as a characteristic of God to an androgynous Mother-and-Fatherhood instead. There is a sense in which this is quite legitimate. Feminine images of God in the Scriptures have for many years been downplayed in favour of masculine ones. By recovering some of these we can begin to get a fuller picture of God's dealings with people, which will challenge the monopoly of male attributes. There is no reason in fact why this should not be an essential part of our understanding of God. Even Christ talks about himself as a 'hen gathering her chicks under her wings' (Matthew 23). God's motherliness is vitally important.

The question is again one of not *whether* we should deepen our understanding of God, but to what extent. For recognizing the scriptural basis for seeing God also as like a mother is a different endeavour from rewriting this into a new doctrine of the Godhead. For to *think* of God in this way would not be enough for many feminists. A much more visible manifestation of our seriousness is required. One such might be to incorporate the 'androgyny' of God into the creeds and the

Lord's prayer: to rewrite the whole Prayer Book in fact with this in mind. We would now find ourselves together praying 'Our Father-and-Mother in heaven, hallowed be your name' or 'In the name of the Father-and-Mother, the Son and the Holy Spirit'. But this has strong doctrinal implications. What has happened to the Trinity? Is God the Father-and-Mother one person or two? The problems this formulation might suggest are as great as the problems it solves. This is why many feminists move away from family connotations altogether, and thereby any 'authoritarianism' and suggest more 'neutral' titles for God: the Holy One, the Almighty Creator, the Source of Love. Whilst these are perfectly acceptable, some others deteriorate into mysticism and impersonality: 'water of life', 'life-giving wind'.

Other feminists in the radical camp object to this pussy-footing about. God is personal, God is familiar, God is loving. Why not simply then reverse the patriarchal package and call God Mother? This title may not be taken up by the Church at large initially, but at least it will provide a focus for a woman-centred spirituality. The Mother-God advocates are therefore a significant voice in the movement. And for many of us there is nothing particularly blasphemous about this position. In a certain sense because God in the end is neither male nor female, if it is helpful for some women to identify with God as the source of all femininity this could be accepted as quite appropriate. Unfortunately in practice that is not where it usually ends. For belief in a Mother-God all too easily moves towards a new understanding of God altogether, one in which the God who discloses himself to us in his revelation is replaced by a god which we devise to meet our needs. Not only that. As far as some Christians are concerned this is only the beginning, 'the first of a whole series of theological dominoes' which, when toppled, will draw down others: 'the incarnation of Christ and the doctrine of grace; the very notion of revelation and the authority of the Bible as the inspired work of God'.[5]

Perhaps then we should pause for a moment to reconsider the problem raised for feminists by the Fatherhood of God. The problem only exists at a deep level because of a flaw in the logic of the initial argument: the equation of God's Fatherhood with maleness. For although to be an earthly and human father is to be undoubtedly male, it does not follow at all that to be God the Father is to be God the Male. God is neither male nor female. Sexuality is a characteristic of creaturehood. It is something which God has *put* in creation. It does not follow either that because God *created* sexuality he must be sexual, any more than because he created time he must be temporal. The confusion is itself one which can affect our very relationship with and experience of God, yet it originates because we take our anthropormophic images too seriously. Maybe the first commandment could have helped us with this.

But there is still more to the issue. For we call God 'Father' because Christ invited us to. And here again, Jesus is not making a point about God's 'gender', nor about his authority even, but is using the word to tell us about the kind of relationship we might have. We might have this intimate, gentle, caring, relationship from one who loves, protects, cuddles, feeds and nourishes us. For the word 'Abba' is nothing like the word used to describe a patriarch. It is simply 'daddy'. Jesus then is inviting us to share his daddy, to come to the relationship with someone who watches our every move, cares about our every tear, and knows exactly where it hurts. To reduce the deep intimacy of this fatherly (and motherly) relationship into fear of a male God is to distance oneself from the source of real self-knowledge and full womanly identity.

Post-Christian feminism

In spite of their feelings of isolation and even alienation most Christian feminists have stayed within the Church, although frequently skirting its edges. Feminist theologians such as Rosemary Radford Ruether have seen their task as one which speaks to the whole Church whilst specifically encouraging women. Yet those who have moved right outside the Church, the 'post-Christian' feminists, continue to exert an influence over many of the remnant. This is because the ideology of sisterhood is greater for many than commitment to the Christian faith. Their struggle as women is seen often as a struggle *against* Christianity instead of a struggle *for* Christianity. It is important then to see how far post-Christian feminism has moved from the gospel of Christ to understand the dangers of identifying as sisters.

Mary Daly was a Catholic theologian, and indeed still teaches theology although she would no longer call herself a Christian. A combination of the maleness of God, the oppression of the Church, and the victimization of women has led her to re-do theology, and go 'beyond God the Father'. Her vision of what is beyond, although for her apparently liberating, is a chilling prospect for feminists who are committed to Christ. Old Christian teachings assume a menacing twist, as they are represented as being derived from an evil patriarchal motivation. The Annunciation, rather than being the amazing disclosure to an ordinary young girl that she will bear the Messiah, is now nothing other than a cosmic rape scene. Similarly the 'Antichrist' now assumes a new form—no longer an evil power, but woman's consciousness, feared certainly by patriarchy because it will herald a new era 'beyond Christolatry into a fuller stage of conscious participation in the *living* God'. The Second Coming is also reinterpreted into this new feminist post-Christian theology: 'The Antichrist and the Second Coming of Women are synonymous. This Second Coming is not a return of Christ but a new arrival of female presence, once strong and powerful, but enchained since the dawn of patriarchy.'[6] And we are back with the goddess. But this is not a personal god(dess). God is 'she', only insofar as 'she' is woman-affirming. In fact, Mary Daly's 'god' is neither personal nor impersonal. Neither 'Father' nor 'Force'. 'God' indeed is not the name of anything at all. Our very problems have so often come about because we have 'reified' God, we have made God into a personal, spiritual or mystical *entity.* But now we need to be liberated from all this. We need to recognize that *God is a Verb:* not Being but Be-ing.

The anthropomorphic symbols for God may be intended to convey personality, but they fail to convey that God is Be-ing. Women who are experiencing the shock of non-being and the surge of self-affirmation against this are inclined to perceive transcendence as the Verb in which we participate—live, move and have our being.[7]

Women's 'becoming' then will usher in the new creation. We shall all *be,* rather than struggle with our non-being in patriarchal society. And this will be salvation. How will it be achieved? Emphatically *not* through any Christ as Saviour:

A patriarchal divinity and His son are exactly *not* able to save us from the horrors of a patriarchal world. Rather, only radical feminism can open up human consciousness adequately to the desire for non-hierarchical, non-oppressive society and reveal sexism as the basic model and source of oppression.[8]

Here we have her doctrine in a nutshell. *Sin is sexism, women are innocent,* and *Christ cannot save.* Only through the women's movement have women any chance at all of liberation.

Although her words are hot and full of passion they fall as an icy shower on the Christian, turning the very blood cold. For not only is the level of apostasy almost incomprehensible, so is the failure to come to terms with the depths of women's problems. Her understanding of women as innocent victims is wrong. As women we participate in the sins of fallen humanity as much as men. What is more, we know we are guilty of sin, not because patriarchal Christianity tells us so, but because we experience sin in our own hearts. We know what it is to hurt someone, to wrong, to judge, to offend, to wound, to hate, to be malicious, unkind and self-centred. That is why sin cannot be identified with sexism, for it is in all of us, and sexism is only one way in which sin functions in our lives and communities. Mary Daly's 'answer' that women who act in evil ways do so as 'token torturers', because they are under some kind of spell of the male sex, is a desperate response. Where does this male sin come from? How do women escape it? Somehow all the blame has to stay with men, even if it takes magic to keep it there.

We cannot follow her path of salvation either. Because we do not simply need to be saved from patriarchy. We need to be saved from our own personal sinfulness. The opening up of women's consciousness, unless it is also accompanied by repentance and turning to God goes only halfway. But such repentance is a million miles off this route. For salvation here is in the end a celebration of womanhood, a rebirth of human consciousness. Freedom is freedom from the restraints of sexism and oppression and patriarchy. This is why the Christian feminist cannot call her 'sister'. For the Christian woman freedom is *freedom in Christ:* free to be human, free to be Christ-like, free to be loving, but *not free to be autonomous.* We cannot go beyond God the Father, Son and

Holy Spirit. *There is no beyond.* Human autonomy, personhood without God, does not exist. God is the very condition of our being. Autonomy is a myth of the Enlightenment, and it is with us still. It can, as we have seen, even seduce those who would call themselves Christians and lead them into very dark places.

Notes

1. Tertullian, *On the Apparel of Women,* book 1, chapter 1, The Ante-Nicene Fathers (Eerdmans 1982), p. 14.
2. William Oddie, *What Will Happen to God?* (SPCK 1984), p. 147.
3. Elizabeth Fiorenza; quoted in Carol Christ, *Womanspirit Rising: A Feminist Reader in Religion* (Harper and Row 1979), p. 147.
4. Paul Moore, *Take a Bishop Like Me* (New York 1979), p. 8.
5. William Oddie, *What Will Happen to God?* p. 26.
6. Mary Daly, *Beyond God the Father* (Boston Press 1973), p. 96.
7. ibid., p. 34.
8. ibid.

PART FOUR
A THIRD WAY

It is now time to open up the tradition which has been absent so far in this book. A biblically Christian feminism which reaches out beyond the institutional Church into all areas of life has a long history. In this section we shall contrast the foundations of all the feminist positions we have looked at so far with this Christian tradition. We follow it through the centuries, focusing particularly on the nineteenth century and on just three of the many areas it affected then. We look at the rationale in Scripture for such a position and ask, If we are to espouse a consciously Christian feminism today what should its concern be?

12: Foundations of Feminism

The Enlightenment

Several times during the last few chapters I have suggested that each of the three branches of feminism which we have examined is part of the same basic tree whose roots ultimately go back to the Enlightenment. I have also made claims that it is this foundation which is ultimately responsible for their failure to come to grips with some of the basic problems of personhood. It is clearly time now to dig more deeply at these roots and exhume the malefactors who have left us this sad legacy.

The eighteenth-century Enlightenment is not so much a historical period as a massive change of direction. It is indeed difficult fully to paint the effect that this period had on the thought-forms, world-view and self-understanding of the age, and I can only use large brushstrokes here to convey a general picture. To understand its effect in a fuller context, it would be good to consult Alan Storkey's packed volume *A Christian Social Perspective.* He sketches the Enlightenment as a movement directed by a *new faith:* 'What then was the content of this new faith? The first basic belief was a *man.* Man was the shaper of his own destiny; he had rights and freedom, and was subject to no higher authority. He was his own source of meaning-coherence; he was autonomous.'[1] This focus on autonomous man, man on his own, man come of age, was the intellectual theme of the age. The whole world had a new look. Society was reappraised. There were debates as to what held societies together, discussions on whether self-interest or benevolence was the chief motivating factor. An acceptance of the basic sinfulness or *depravity* of man was replaced by a belief in the natural goodness of the human race. 'Nature' was venerated, bringing an emphasis on natural law, natural justice, natural theology, natural rights and undergirding it all, the *natural light of reason.* The prevailing concept of God was that of the deist: a god whom we can know about through nature, a god who set the universe in motion and then modestly retired to let it tick on according to these natural laws. It was not, of course, followed by an immediate popular rejection of Christianity, although there was a growth in the Unitarian Church. It was more that the Enlightenment thinkers moved the basis of belief in God on to a different plane, away from revelation and on to nature and reason, with huge implications. Christ's atonement, for example, makes little sense when people are naturally good, and evil is mostly caused by ignorance and superstition.

Reason, then, was to be the arbiter, personal freedom the goal and natural rights the rationale for the new era. The influence was everywhere. The American Declaration of Independence in 1776 embodied some of this Enlightenment faith in the natural and inalienable rights of man. The last decade of the century saw the French revolutionary movement, through the writings of Thomas Paine, brought into the arena of natural rights. In 1791 – 2 Paine published his *Rights of Man*. But the optimism of the Enlightenment was on the wane, to be delivered a crushing blow by the Revolution bloodbath when Reason, after all, was not apparently much good as an arbiter. And yet a new development within it was just beginning. Along with renewed interest in the rights of *man* came an awakening to the rights of *women*. Indeed, why not? If there were no divinely ordained or revealed differences between men and women, if they were part of the common rationality of humanity, what was the reason for one sex to be denied the privileges, status, education and legal rights of the other sex? Why was one sex so readily subjugated by the other? It could only be on the grounds of physical weakness, but this was not reason enough. Mary Wollstonecraft wrote her *Vindication of the Rights of Women* in 1792. Nor was she alone. Amongst others, the French revolutionary, 'Olympe' de Gouge had made her own *Declaration of The Rights of Women* three years earlier. Gouge received no thanks from her male revolutionary colleagues, incidentally, for she along with a group of like-minded others, was guillotined as a counter-revolutionary.

So the influence of the Enlightenment on the development of liberal feminism is evident immediately. Individual liberty, natural rights, and the dictates of reason have left their still visible imprint on liberal feminism up to this day. Yet the influence was not restricted to this group. In a more fundamental way still, the idea of human *autonomy,* personhood-without-God, is the starting point of both Marxists[2] and radicals. For 'freedom' means woman unshackled; woman *with no higher authority.* This is seen as under the authority of neither man nor God: woman on her own. And although for the mainstream Enlightenment this obsession was with man's autonomy, rather than with woman's, the roots of radicalism are here. Mankind was *free:* free to do what was right in its own understanding, and in harmony with nature. Nature and freedom were the twin themes of the Enlightenment.

Nature *and* freedom?

Those of you who are familiar with some of the philosophical debates in contemporary social science may feel that rush of recognition here. For as well as being the source of the ideas of woman's autonomy, the Enlightenment is also the source of an unresolvable dilemma which has appeared throughout the account of feminism so far. It is not confined to the issue of feminism either. For the determinist free-will debate, the debate between the behaviourists and the action theorists, the neo-Freudians and the existentialists all comes from this basic issue of the relationship between nature and freedom. 'Man was born free' cried Rousseau in 1762,[3] 'but everywhere he is in chains.' Who made the chains? asks the sceptic. If it is merely the system which corrupts who devised the system? Man is on his own after all and can devise what he wishes.

So much of contemporary social science is fundamentally a matter of taking sides on this dilemma. The quarrel is between those who start from the assumption that we can have no real freedom of choice because we are in some sense 'determined', products of our environment, our biology, our culture, our class, our upbringing, our psyche, and those who maintain that our very humanity lies in the fact of our freedom. We cannot be fully human unless we are free. It all arises from the Enlightenment attempt to marry nature with freedom *whilst at the same time rejecting the Christian foundation which holds them together.* For dependency, creatureliness, being subject to norms, whether biological, social, economic, legal or ethical is the real human condition. Freedom comes not from 'transcending' dependency, from trying to go 'beyond' God the Father to human autonomy, but from recognizing

our human createdness and discovering God's own norms for
our institutional, social, economic and personal lives. It is not
more 'free' for a violin to be played with a drumstick. It would
either produce an awful noise or wreck the violin. If we want
it to be itself we play it with the bow that was made for it. If
we want to be human we live according to what has been
designed as in our best interests. Freedom comes from
following the Maker's instructions. Without that recognition
the dilemma of nature or freedom will resurface, unresolved,
until the starting-point is finally abandoned. Meanwhile, the
dilemma is present in the very articulation of the struggles of
contemporary feminism. Does my biological *nature* determine
my destiny or can I really be *free?* How can lesbianism be
contrary to *nature* when *freedom* brings open sexual relations?
How can I break *free* from the chains of nature, the class
system, the patriarchal culture and be myself? Again, who
made the chains? Apparently, free people.

One other point here is important. For although to the
feminists men made the chains, we would not want to
exonerate women from responsibility here too. Both women
and men together are implicated, and together have
contributed to the problems of contemporary society. They
may not, of course, be *equally* to blame for clearly in the
situations we have examined men have the greater guilt on
their shoulders. They have dominated, controlled, manipulated, abused and shackled women, exploiting their
vulnerability and weakness. But women are not the Innocents.
Their greed, indulgence, and selfishness contributed also to
the injustice of the class system, and the deprivations of the
nineteenth and twentieth centuries. Nor have some of them
been slow to use *their* ability to seduce, manipulate and
exploit men sexually. Women through the ages have not, any
more than men, been primarily motivated by love, care or
desire for justice. The fact that they have been the ones more
easily injured and more frequently repressed and subjugated
is indeed an indictment of male attitudes, and even the
patriarchal system, but it does not absolve women from their
own sins. For this is where the Enlightenment perspective
still blurs the vision of contemporary feminism. The espousal
of autonomy meant a rejection of depravity. The deep
humanist faith in (wo)man was faith in a basically *good*
humanity. Clearly, if depravity were real, rather than

imagined, it would greatly limit our freedom. Yet the biblical message that we are sinful is the only one which can account for the situations we experience around us. Depravity is real enough: we are slaves to ourselves and will enslave whichever others we can put under our power. The final irony remains that in turning their back on sin these writers have turned their back on forgiveness too, and through forgiveness on the *possibility of freedom*. For freedom to love, to cherish, to grow, to be honest, to receive love, to be myself all comes from knowing who I am, and knowing that my sins have been dealt with: they no longer dominate me, and in a deep sense no matter who else might oppress me I am free.

So, although we recognize that the fight for justice and against inequality is a real one, it neither starts nor finishes with a declaration of human autonomy. Attempted autonomy in itself constitutes the very heart of the problem. We need, then, to turn from the Enlightenment and find a firmer base for our fight; one which has a much more realistic understanding of what it is to be human.

Biblically-inspired feminism

Several times I have referred in passing to feminists who cannot be identified with any of the major branches outlined so far. In the chapter on feminism in the Church we put aside those feminists who would call themselves biblical Christians. Similarly we noted but did not dwell on those feminists in the nineteenth century who were characterized by a committed Christian view of men and women. Now it is time to consider this tradition. For there are feminists who do not take their cue from the autonomy of the Enlightenment but from a Christian view of people-under-God: a view which recognizes the reality of sin and the need of salvation. But it is not an individualist belief, for salvation does not simply affect 'personal' or 'moral' life, but needs to be worked out in fear and trembling in all areas, including that of sex and gender.

The Reformation

The Christian feminist tradition has roots longer than those derived from the Enlightenment faith. The Reformation itself provided a remarkable impetus for a redefining of woman's place. This is not to say that the Reformation writers were themselves feminists, any more than the Enlightenment or early Marxist theorists would claim that term. For all three the reverse is more often true. John Knox's *First Blast of the Trumpet against the Monstrous Regiment of Women,* although a little excited in its language, was not outlandish in its day. At the same time many of the other reformers were not nearly so misogynist as we might believe. Luther and Calvin went to some pains to refute the then held Catholic belief that women were inevitably unclean and agents of the devil. To break with the medieval suspicion of sex was liberating in itself, moving as it did from the idea that virginity was always morally superior to marriage. Calvin went further still, stressing the companionable aspect to marriage rather than marriage as a means of procreation. Not surprisingly, this new outlook produced a break also from arranged marriages, where the daughter was often merely a part of a familial bargaining process, to marriage based on personal choice and personal commitment. The reformers regulated the marriage laws themselves to apply to both men and women. Divorce on the grounds of proven adultery was obtainable for *either* partner: a reform not on the English statute books until 1923!

Yet important though these details are they would not in themselves produce a rationale for Christian feminism. Far more important for this were the central doctrines of the Reformation. For with the denial of papal authority, and the limiting of the authority of the bishops the Reformation stressed the mediation of Christ alone, and the responsibility of each person before God. 'Each person' included women. Luther himself saw men and women as together made in God's image, and as such to be equal in the order of redemption. In his emphasis on the depravity of mankind Calvin included both men and women, and saw too both men and women as part of God's plan for salvation. The priesthood of all believers replaced the notion of the priesthood of the special few. All human beings, whatever their sin, whatever their sex, could have direct contact with God through Jesus Christ. So although men and women might occupy different roles and offices in temporal society there was no distinction between them in the eyes of God. They were heirs together: joint-heirs in Christ.

It is easy to see how this new liberating theology led to a reawakening of women to their own situation. Women were no longer basically inferior. God himself had said that in Christ there was no male nor female, but that all were one. With the Bible now available in the language of the people women had a new reason for wanting education. The responsibility for understanding and obeying God's truth was now upon them, and not on a professional male mediator whose word they could not question. Two historians surveying the position of women through many periods summarize the effect of the protestant changes. '[They] emphasised in one way or another a personal, non-hierarchical, lay-dominated religion that looked to Scripture for its authority. In such a movement women would find a place.'5 A growing awareness of this place was evident in seventeenth-century Puritanism. The influence of this committed and earnest group of people was felt not only in the area of Christian doctrine, but in science, law and business. In Puritan homes girls were often educated along with their brothers, and it was a period which saw a growing interest of women in theology. For theology was no longer just the queen of the sciences fit only for the company of male princes; it could now keep company with anyone who believed. Godly women wrote tracts, organized women's study groups and Bible-reading sessions. Some Protestant groups, such as the Quakers, endorsed the right of women to preach and teach. In Puritan America women in other churches, Presbyterian and Independent, were allowed to hold office and, also important, saw a great extension to their spheres of activity in work and business. The Reformation had opened up the issue of the place of women and had provided through its world and life view the dynamic for Christian feminists of the future. This was to be realized in strength in the nineteenth century when Christian women were activated into energetic and reformist campaigns of a fervour and depth not previously encountered.

Nineteenth-century evangelical feminism
Evangelical revivals are often dismissed as being pietist and otherworldly. They are seen as associated with a reactionary morality and an unhealthy obsession with sin. For these reasons they are regarded as unpromising conditions for the development of new social insights. Conversely, those

Christians who become very deeply involved in social and political affairs have sometimes been labelled by pietist Christians as 'social gospellers'. Their Christian understanding has become defined by and absorbed into a social or political framework. However, the Evangelical feminists of the nineteenth century were neither otherworldly pietists nor social gospellers. For the same Evangelical movement which heightened awareness of God in the late eighteenth and early nineteenth centuries also produced in some a deep social conscience which was to have repercussions for many decades. Salvation did not imply simply the saving of individual souls. It involved also stressing the dignity of men and women created by God, and the fight against social and structural sin. It is now well documented that significant among these areas of concern was a concern for justice for women. The drive for justice was to encompass not just the moral and domestic issues, but many areas new on the agenda of Christian women: issues such as education, employment, better wages and conditions, the abolition of slavery and justice for the prostitute. The enlarging scope of the New York Moral Reform Society summarizes the development of the Evangelical feminist outlook. Initially evangelistic, the society became involved in moral reform and finally in broader political and social issues. By 1860 women's suffrage was already being advocated. The evangelical journal *The Advocate of Moral Reform* followed a similar development. Edited and controlled by women, the journal had, by the 1850s, become a mouthpiece of feminist concerns, challenging even the most sacred idea that a woman's only happiness came through marriage.

Nor were these interests limited to American women. Although there was something of a time lag, British Christians too began to move into the same areas of concern and take up often mammoth battles against the male establishment. Some of the women pioneers suffered ostracism and rebuff at the hands of fellow Christians and found then, as now, that rather than rely on support from the mainstream of the Church, they had to work with others who did not share their Christian outlook. Thus, although Christian in their inception and inspiration, many of these campaigns drew in also feminists from an Enlightenment individualist perspective.

One theme which remained constant in this early Christian

feminism was a commitment to *others*. Mostly, these women were not fighting for their own case. It was not *their* rights, employment, need for justice which drove them, but concern for those who were weak and oppressed: those at the fag ends of respectable society who could not present their own case. This is why it would be utterly wrong to dismiss these women as simply middle class. Only middle-class Christians could have spearheaded the changes which took place during this century, and then at considerable cost to themselves. On one issue at least the support was far wider than this anyway, as we shall now consider. I have chosen to look at just three of the many programmes involving Christian feminists: slavery, temperance and prostitution, because each of these challenged entrenched economic and male interests.

Slavery

It is no coincidence that the most flagrant and influential anti-slavery novel was written by a Christian and a woman.[6] For although Harriet Beecher Stowe's name was singled out for condemnation in the Southern States, she was not alone in her position. The involvement of Christian women in the abolition movement has by now been well documented. (Heasman 1962, Lerner 1967, Scott 1970, Melder 1977, Evans 1979, Banks 1981.) Nor did the movement stop with middle-class whites, such as the Grimké sisters, who had witnessed the ugliness of slavery as daughters of a Southern slave owner. (Angelina Grimké's pamphlet *An Appeal to the Christian Women of the South* was burned in her home city.) Former slaves themselves made a huge contribution. The story of Harriet Tubman and the underground railroad has been told over and over again. Sojourner Truth was another freed slave whose Christian zeal took her through the country to urge and persuade people of the implications of the gospel for the abolition of slavery. She was a formidable opponent and, though illiterate, reached thousands with her message. The same Christian motivation was found in women from the North-east and Mid-west. Lucy Stone, an educated girl born in Massachusetts, was urged not to get involved in the abolition movement. Her response was simple: 'If, in this hour of the world's need I should refuse to lend my aid, however small it may be, I should have no right to think myself a Christian.'[7] Antoinette Brown was another committed American Christian who lent her aid to the cause. In England, as in the US, Quaker women played a prominent part. However, what is particularly significant for us is that many of these same women were to become vanguards of the feminist movement. Quite early on a strong link was forged between the emancipation of slaves and the emancipation of women. Lucy Stone had gone to college to study Greek and Hebrew, anxious to see for herself whether the passages on women's submission in the Scriptures had been correctly translated. Sarah Grimké's views were already quite radical by 1837 when she declared that 'whatever it is morally right for a man to do it is morally right for a woman to do.'[8] Antoinette Brown tried to have a resolution introduced in 1852 which declared that women's rights were upheld by the Bible. Sojourner Truth too turned her attention to women's emancipation alongside the abolition cause, and became equally fervent in her speeches and addresses on this subject, and equally convinced that her authority and inspiration were God himself. In 1838 Angelina Grimké was writing in public letters to Catherine Beecher, a woman's educationalist but critical of the strident activity of the Grimkés: 'The discussion of the rights of slaves has opened the way for the discussion of other rights, and the ultimate result will be most certainly the breaking of every yoke . . . emancipation far more glorious than the world has ever yet seen.'[9]

Nor were these women slow to practise their beliefs in their personal lives. Lucy Stone and Antoinette Brown married the sympathetic Blackwell brothers, one of whose sisters was the pioneer woman doctor. Henry Blackwell promised Lucy 'perfect equality' in their marriage, and their joint protest at the marriage laws extended to Lucy's retaining even her own surname. Their strong, faithful, supportive relationship and family life showed that marriage was based on something principally deeper than ownership and legal possession. In his marriage to Angelina Grimké, Theodore Weld gave up all his legal rights to his wife's property. Simplifying the vows they made to each other, Angelina promised to love him 'with a pure heart fervently'.[10] The five Blackwell sisters remained single, but interestingly each adopted a daughter to carry on their ideas.

It is probably important to note here that although there was a cross current between Christianity, the abolition movement and feminism, there were many in each category who would not identify with the other groups. Just as the abolition movement had split the churches, women's rights split the anti-slavery movement. In Britain the link between feminism and abolition was weaker anyway, except among Quaker women such as Anne Knight. The Evangelical Clapham Sect, one of the earliest groups to take on the anti-slavery campaign, included both William Wilberforce and Hannah More. Neither of these would have claimed any involvement with a feminist movement, although Hannah More spent much of her life, after her conversion, in educating women, and particularly poor women. But in 1804 for an Evangelical to adopt the stance taken even fifty years later would have been seen as a stumbling block to believers. As it was, by the 1840s the feminist abolitionists in the US were proving an embarrassment to the movement, and were being asked to modify or suppress their specifically feminist opinions. Angelina Grimké herself acknowledged some regret that the issue of women's rights was emerging before the abolition of slavery had been achieved. She nevertheless consoled herself with the belief that it 'must be the Lord's time and therefore the *best* time.'[11] However, most of the abolitionist men did not agree with her, and what happened next was to be repeated in a still more dramatic and radical way 120 years later.

The anti-slavery movement edged away from individual campaigning and *ad hoc* public meetings to national and world conventions. Although women held their own conventions they were in fact excluded from the World Convention in London in 1840. In many ways this marked the end of their usefulness in the abolition movement, for the efforts of the male campaigners now shifted to Congress. Clearly women had no vote and no part to play in the political lobbying which was to mark events from now on. For some women this meant their job had been done. For those who had been drawn into a feminist position it meant their job had been frustrated. Their lack of any political status denied them the right to do all they wanted to end slavery. A historical all women's gathering was held in Seneca Falls, New York, in 1848. It would have looked strange to modern eyes. Women in quaint Quaker dress, happily married wives, mothers of large families, former slaves and educated girls

comprised indeed a very different group from the organization
of 'divorced wives, childless women and sour old maids'
described derisively by one newspaper columnist. Radical
women with a Christian heartbeat stood alongside those of
an Enlightenment position, and together formally embraced a
new cause. The international woman's suffrage movement
had come into being.

Temperance

The temperance societies of the nineteenth century bring a
smile to many faces. They are often regarded as quaint and
moralistic. It comes as no surprise to these people to learn
that they were a product of Evangelical Christianity. However,
what sometimes does come as surprising is that they were
also the spawning ground for feminism.

It was not simply a moral distaste for drunkenness which
produced the temperance campaigns. Far more was involved
than that. Alcohol, particularly in the more concentrated
form then available, was closely associated with economic
hardship, family ruin, wife abuse and prostitution. Given the
economic dependence of wives and the absence of legal rights
for women, a man who spent all his money on drink could
reduce his entire family to poverty or even starvation, and his
wife was powerless to take action against it. A more sinister
feature still was the tie-up between alcohol, the gambling
den, the brothel and the employer. In many American towns
drink perpetuated 'boss rule'. Sexual abuse from husbands,
poverty and hunger forced many women and their daughters
into prostitution. Some were even 'sold' to brothel owners to
pay off drink and gambling debts. In this context the
temperance movement becomes no longer amusing but one
serious way of attacking the utter vulnerability of wives and
children, and even of men themselves. A later way was of
course to change the legal underpinning itself.

So although not all temperance workers were feminists
almost all feminists supported temperance at some stage.
Sarah and Angelina Grimké, Lucy Stone and Elizabeth
Blackwell all gave it their support in those early years. Susan
Anthony, again from a Quaker background and later to
become one of America's leading suffrage workers, began her
feminism in the temperance movement. However, the
campaign was to be a long one, stretching from the 1830s

into the twentieth century. For like the abolition movement the prohibitionists were challenging powerful economic interests which were not ready to see any diminution of profits without a struggle. So, even though prohibition was accepted in some of the states by the 1860s, it was frequently abandoned again. In 1869 the Women's Christian Temperance Union had formed in the US and, more than the numerous counterparts in Britain, was to have a hidden agenda. A new generation of feminists had become involved by the 1870s. Frances Willard, a strong Christian woman, had become converted to suffrage through temperance, and became president of this Union. She and the Reverend Anna Shaw bridged the chasm which still seperated women of the Church from the suffrage cause. Anna Shaw enlisted the help of Evangelical church ministers and was to forge an alliance in the Mid-west between the Evangelical churches, temperance and suffrage. By the 1890s the aggressive Anti-Saloon League had been formed. The brigades of Christian women who went from saloon to saloon with Bible in one hand and hatchet in the other presented a very formidable presence! If biblical argument did not prevail then the axe would and, rather than see their bars wrecked by hoards of chopping women, many publicans would rush to pour whisky down the drain.

For the most part, however, the methods were publicity and persuasion. Frances Willard was undoubtedly a skilful and careful leader for the movement. A safe, conservative Christian, she would use the Temperance Union as the organization to advocate progressive legislation, child labour laws and women's suffrage. Her appeal always found the ear of her listeners because even the most radical measure was advocated in the name of purity and the home.

The temperance workers were treated to no greater respect than the abolitionists had been. They were frequently dismissed as 'only women', and hence of no significance even though their organization numbered almost a quarter of a million members. By the time the Prohibition Amendment was passed the temperance cause had educated three generations of women in raising social consciousness and agitating for reform.

Concern for women and families in poverty, neglect, hardship and brutality had thus taken Christian women up to the very point of two amendments to the Constitution of the United States, or indeed three, if their contribution towards the abolition of slavery in 1865 is included here. The development from temperance to feminist legislation is an indisputable one. A contemporary writer commented: 'They have mixed those babies up, and women's suffrage and temperance are not merely foster brothers but twins, and look so much alike you don't know which is which.'[12] What is more, a study of twenty-six suffrage leaders between 1890 and 1920 found not only a strong link between the older ones and the Women's Christian Temperance Union, it also discovered that twenty-five of them were Protestants. Although there was now a marked difference between them and the Evangelical feminists who had gone before, the Christian legacy had been a long one.

Prostitution

So far, this account of the outworking of the Reformation perspective in nineteenth-century feminism has leaned mostly on American examples. In this next issue, our focus will be on Britain. For, although concern for the prostitute was evident among such women as Lucy Stone and Frances Willard, it was British Christians who took on a massive battle against legislation imposed on suspected prostitutes. Again, it was not simply individual rights which were at stake; it was a challenge hurled against the dual standard of sexual behaviour, against patriarchal interests which defined morality from a male vantage point, against economic abuse and deprivation which forced many women into prostitution, and against laws which condemned sin in women but condoned it in men.

The Contagious Diseases Acts were passed quietly in Britain in 1864, 1866 and 1869, each Act extending the scope of the previous one. By 1869 they were applicable in eighteen towns in Britain where there was a heavy concentration of personnel from the armed services. They were designed to protect soldiers and sailors from venereal disease, not by making prostitution illegal, but by checking prostitutes. To this end any woman suspected of being a prostitute was required to undergo a regular medical examination to detect and then treat VD. Feminists reacted to the Acts immediately, but were largely ignored until 1869 when there was a move to extend them to other parts of the country.

A national association for the repeal of the Acts, spearheaded initially by a group of Christian men, approached Josephine Butler to take up the campaign. She was an excellent choice. Already an active supporter of better education for women and women's suffrage it was her work with prostitutes in Liverpool which had given her unparalleled insights into the relationship between poverty and prostitution. Her view of prostitutes as *victims,* both of the dual standard of sexual morality and of discriminatory economic structures, made her campaign a very human one. As a committed Christian, and thus as much against sin and vice as any other Victorian, Josephine Butler detested the hypocrisy which the Act manifested. With the full support of her husband she agreed to lead the campaign, though knowing full well the possible outcome for her husband's position in the Church. Her misgivings were not unfounded. Feminists from a wide range of positions, Quakers, Evangelicals and those right outside the Church, were quick to lend their support. *The Women's Protest* in 1870 included the signatures of Florence Nightingale, Mary Carpenter and Harriet Martineau.

What was it about the Contagious Diseases Acts which were so objectionable? Surely the eradication of venereal disease was a reasonable aim? Jacob Bright (also a supporter of woman's suffrage) summed up the anger against them on 20 July, 1870. It was, he claimed, 'a law passed by peers and prelates in one chamber, and by an assembly of rich men in another, the whole burden of which is directed against the poor women of the country'. He argued that women 'frightened by the police are induced to sign their names or put their crosses to a paper the meaning of which they know nothing'. From then on they were subjected to fortnightly examinations (defined as 'physical rape') which were often very painful, and always humiliating. Five objections to the law were raised, some of which have a curiously modern ring about them. Too many discretionary powers were given to the police; the Acts were directed against the poorer classes who were uneducated and particularly vulnerable; they discriminated solely against women and not against the male clients who might themselves be responsible for the spread of

VD; poor homes could be entered and women who had never been prostitutes could be subjected to this painful ordeal; finally, the Acts failed anyway in checking the disease.

It was the *injustice* of the Acts, however, rather than their failure which concerned the campaigners. Nor were they satisfied with the counter-argument used to justify the unequal treatment of men and women. Apparently there was 'no comparison to be made between prostitutes and the men who consort with them'. But surely both were involved in the same act? The Act's defenders dismissed this, because it had a different meaning for each party. For the women it was a matter of vice and financial gain. For the men it was merely the 'irregular indulgence of a natural impulse'. This contrasted sharply with the views of Josephine Butler. She felt simply that the Acts degraded and violated women. They were not at all concerned for the health and welfare of the prostitute herself, nor even for finding ways of helping her away from prostitution. They saw her only as an object for men's 'irregular indulgence'. The Acts existed *for the benefit of men,* of soldiers and sailors, but they were applied solely against the woman. They tried in fact to turn such a woman into 'a vessel periodically cleaned for public use'.[13]

How humiliating and hurtful the experience was for women was illustrated by the case of Mrs Percy. Not a prostitute, and not carrying any venereal disease, she was apprehended nevertheless and forced to undergo the examination. But the trauma of the whole unpleasant experience was too much for her, and she committed suicide.

The first success for the campaign had come in opposing a government candidate who supported the Acts. He foolishly went on record as regretting that the Act did not include provisions for examining the wives of service personnel themselves. Since his constituency included many service families, this did not endear him to the electorate . He was defeated, and the extension of the Acts did not continue. However, the successes of the 1870s were few, and the leaders were subjected to ostracism and rebuff, both from church leaders and from other suffragists who felt this campaign would turn public opinion against them. In the 1880s, Josephine Butler's work developed into a wider crusade against child prostitution, and exposed some horrifying details. The publication of Stead's *Maiden Tribute to Modern Babylon* showed conclusively that for very many women prostitution was not a matter of choice. 'Sold' to brothel owners at a very young age, this was all that many of the girls had ever known. Destitution and poverty, kidnappings and orphanhood left many children with no means of protection. Young girls would be sexually abused 'in exchange for meat pies'. The public outcry which followed Stead's revelations ensured the repeal of the Contagious Diseases Acts in 1886.

The motivation and inspiration of these Christian women of the nineteenth century was in many ways quite straightforward. They believed in the dignity of the person. Women and men, created by a loving God, were to be respected as such, and not oppressed, abused and manipulated by those who had power and institutionalized self-interest on their side. The dignity of women had been particularly under threat, for women were vulnerable economically, socially, and legally. The dual standard was particularly abhorrent to them, not because it deprived a certain class of individuals of their equality, but because it condoned sin in one sex and punished it in the other. It is interesting that in wanting an end to the double standard they were not advocating more sexual permissiveness for women, but greater restraint for men. 'Votes for women and purity for men' was one of the earliest suffragette slogans! More than this, however, these women were motivated by *compassion*, whether for the slave, the poverty-stricken mother or the prostitute. Far from a self-righteous moralism which often characterizes views of this period, they were prepared to face great unpopularity, and rejection from fellow-Christians, in order to act upon what they believed in. They were prepared to identify with the abused and discarded in society, in a way which simply followed the footsteps of Christ himself. I believe that it is with this tradition that Christian feminists of today must compare themselves. Humility, love, compassion, concern for those weak and oppressed, and willingness to suffer, is a difficult agenda to take on board.

Notes

1. A. J. Storkey, *A Christian Social Perspective* (Inter-varsity Press 1979), p. 27.
2. ibid., p. 61.
3. J. J. Rousseau, *The Social Contract and Discourses* (Everyman 1973), p. 3.
4. 1923 Matrimonial Causes Act.
5. Renate Bridenthal and Claudia Koonz, *Becoming Visible: Women in European History* (London, Miffin, 1977), p. 169.
6. Harriet Beecher Stowe, *Uncle Tom's Cabin.*
7. Alice Stone Blackwell, *Lucy Stone, Pioneer of Women's Rights* (Boston 1930), p. 66.
8. Sarah Grimké, *Letters on the Equality of the Sexes and the Condition of Women* (Boston 1838), *Faces of Feminism* p. 21.
9. Gerder Lerner, *The Grimké Sisters From South Carolina: Rebels Against Slavery.* Houghton Mifflin 1967.
10. Andrew Sinclair, *The Better Half* (Jonathan Cape 1966), p. 47.
11. ibid., p. 45.
12. ibid., p. 224. Quoted from Lois Merh, *Massachusetts and the Woman Suffrage Movement.* Thesis in Radcliffe Library 1961.
13. Constance Rover, *Love, Morals and the Feminists* (Routledge and Kegan Paul 1970), pp. 76−8. See also, Dale Spender (ed.), *Feminist Theorists, 3 Centuries of Women's Intellectual Tradition* (Women's Press 1983), pp. 146−64. Other books used in this chapter are R. Evans, *The Feminists* (Croom Helm 1979); K. Heasman, *Evangelicals in Action* (Bles. 1962); K. Melder, *Beginnings of Sisterhood* (Schocken 1977); and A. Scott, *The Southern Lady* (University of Chicago Press 1970).

13: Women, Men and The Bible

Offering an alternative tradition of Christian feminism does not mean that the relationship between Christianity and feminism has now been resolved. For the tradition itself might not after all be as biblically based as we hope. There are many Christians who will remain unconvinced until the biblical teaching itself is assessed because the simple scriptural texts seem to indicate a male—female hierarchy. The time has clearly now come to focus on the Scriptures themselves, and ask what they do teach about men and women that is conclusive. The examination will necessarily not go into great textual depth for these issues have been discussed at length in other writings, and for a more thorough analysis I would urge the reader to consult these.[1]

In the chapter on women and the Church we saw that asserting what the Bible 'says' on a contemporary issue always involves us in some hermeneutical principles. 'What is the purpose of this passage?' 'What was the author's intention here?' 'Is this a timeless truth, or wise counsel for a specific occasion?' 'To whom is this written?' 'What were the social conditions of the time?' 'What heresy is being addressed here?' All these are important preliminary questions. Investigating the biblical text also means of course coming to terms with the language. For God chose to reveal his truth to us in human language, and we must respect all the different and dynamic aspects of such language. Language changes and develops within a certain culture, so that words and phrases within a given culture have certain connotations. We have to be sure that we understand therefore not just the translated words, but the syntax, morphology, context and idioms of the original. It is so easy to bring to the Scriptures our own ideas based on a contemporary use of words and then read these back into the text. We have to recognize too that the meaning of certain texts is by no means clear (1 Corinthians 11 verse 10, 1 Timothy 2 verse 15). As one writer puts it: 'It is possible to know the meaning of all the words in a particular sentence and still have difficulty understanding the meaning of the sentence.'[2] The widespread disagreement over the meaning of 'headship' illustrates this well.[3]

Another big issue is what relative weight we give to different teachings in the Bible. We can be greatly in danger of getting some themes way out of perspective. Even those who take (wrongly in my view) an authoritarian view of the relation between men and women need also to recognize that in the light of other biblical truths this is insignificant anyway. Far deeper issues about the relationship between men and women are at stake than that of who makes the (somewhat mythical) 'final decision'. Far more crucial is the teaching on love: self-giving and self-denying love which should characterize all relationships. More crucial too is the teaching on truth in relationships, on faithfulness, justice, troth, forgiveness and reconciliation. The way others will know that we are Christ's disciples is in the way we love one another, and not in the way we exercise authority over one another.

Finally, for our purposes, is the whole question of how we read the Scriptures in relation to contemporary social issues. Do we, for example, take the Mosaic Law as our paradigm and try to rebuild contemporary society on an Old Testament model? Or do we look for 'biblical principles' which can be extrapolated from all the detailed teachings of both Old and New Testaments and incorporated into a modern programme? Do we see those structures as outlined in some of Paul's epistles as being necessary for a healthy society (with the exception of slavery) or do we focus on Jesus's ministry and see all social life as the detailed outworking of *agape?* Should we finally try to extrapolate 'creation norms' from the Bible and see them as central in understanding how to live, or develop 'kingdom principles' focusing on life in the Spirit? Not all of these are mutually exclusive of course, although each of them is advocated in a variety of perspectives. But they all make some assumptions about the development of Scripture and the development of society which need to be made explicit. Before we commit ourselves to one or more of these approaches I feel a prior suggestion might be to step back further still to see some of the main themes of the whole of Scripture. With this broad canvas in front of us we might be more able to work out better the context and perspective of the individual bits. 'What the Bible says about women' might then be seen in a different light when we do not simply concentrate on specific texts in isolation.

Creation, fall and redemption
The theme of creation, fall and redemption undergirds most others in the Scriptures. It encompasses the disclosure of God as creator, the meaning of humanness, the rejection of God's norms and a turning to sin, and the coming of Christ to buy back those who are his. It is the theme which displays the *covenant* God, the theme which inspires much of Milton's *Paradise Lost* and *Paradise Regained.* In understanding it we can begin to understand how radically different a Christian view of the person is from any secular humanist view. Because the theme discloses three different stages it is helpful to see how the relationship between woman and man is presented at each stage.

Creation
The Bible mentions woman in the very first chapter of Genesis. Right away we learn a number of crucial factors. Woman is one half of mankind, and is created by God. She is made as a being distinct from the animals, but together with man stands on the pinnacle of God's creation. More than this, man and woman together make up the image of God. There is another interesting point. 'Man' in the Genesis account stands for 'humanity' and not for a person with a specific gender attribute. 'So God created man in his own image, in the image of God he created him, male and female he created them.' The frequent Old and New Testament references to 'man' usually have this in mind. They are talking of *man* as distinct from *God, angels,* or *animals,* not as man as distinct from *woman.* Nor are they necessarily assuming that the 'man' will be male.

Not only are man and woman together created in the image of God they are also given joint responsibilities over the rest of creation. Together they are told to have dominion over everything else, and to exercise stewardship. Sexual differences are built into the man—woman relationship: they are made 'male and female', and are given the job of producing children. However, nothing in the first chapter of Genesis would support any hierarchical view of man and woman. Whatever applies to one applies equally to the other.

In Genesis 2 there is a more detailed account where the order of creation is mentioned. The man was created first, and the woman created from the man to be his 'helper'. Many have taken this to suggest that the position of woman is therefore an inferior one. However, this is stretching the account too far. It is certainly not possible to read a superiority for the male because he was created before the woman. The reverse argument would hold equally well, that as the creation proceeded from lower to higher forms of life the woman as the last created was the most sublime. Also the notion of 'helper' is still misunderstood. Many have pointed out that *ezer* ('help', 'helper': Genesis 2.18) is never used in the Old Testament of someone who is an inferior or less able being. Mostly the word is used with reference to God himself.

The creation of man and woman thus embodies three features: equality, diversity and unity. They are made equals, sharing together a distinctiveness from the animals and sharing together in the image of God. They are made different, complementing each other's sexuality with different reproductive functions. They are made to be together, united as 'one flesh', together as the two halves of mankind and providing companionship for each other.

Fall

Most of the destructive power relationships between the sexes which we have observed in this book were not part of the original creation of man and woman, but came as a result of sin. The two sexes are portrayed as originally living in harmony with God, each other and the rest of creation, but with disobedience came distortion. The theme of Genesis 3 is thus the theme of spoiled relationships. Sin altered the innocence of the egalitarian man—woman, husband—wife relationship of creation. The wife now becomes more vulnerable: her childbearing role will now be accompanied by much more pain. In turn the husband becomes dominant: he will 'rule over' her. The results are very much what has been documented in man—woman relationships throughout the ages. But they were not part of the initial structure. Luther comments: 'Had Eve not sinned she would have raised children without any pain or sorrow. Nor would she have been subject to her husband.'[4] Many contemporary theologians see it the same way. Thielicke argues that the rule of man over woman is 'not an imperative order of creation but rather the element of disorder that disturbs the original peace'.[5]

A crucial question is whether this was now to be the new normative structure for marriage, and possibility for all male—female relationships, or whether it was simply a prediction of what would happen because of sin. If it is the former, then it is difficult to understand some of Jesus's attitudes and teaching in the New Testament. If it is the latter, then we should look to the New more than to the Old Testament for teaching on what the new relationship would be like when sin is conquered and the kingdom ushered in.

Redemption

Sin had spoiled the relationship of woman and man to each other but it did not end it. The image was marred but not destroyed. Humankind was alienated but not abandoned, and God himself was to heal that alienation by the redemptive act of Christ. Jesus was to die for our sins, restore us to the Father and give us life in abundance (Romans 10.9; 1 Peter 2.24; John 10.10). In this new kingdom, this age of redemption, those who are his people do not therefore need to live in the old order: there is healing and freedom in the Spirit which has implications for the whole of our lives. For Don Wilson, this incorporates the woman—man relationship: 'Since one of the consequences of Adam's sin was the development of a dominant—submissive relationship that was foreign to the character of male—female relationships in Creation, the redemptive work of Christ will affect the nature of those relationships. Christ's work will have a restorative or corrective influence in this area.'[6]

How do we know what the implications of redemption are for our lives together? Galatians 3.28 is the most frequently quoted passage in this context: 'So there is no difference between Jews and Gentiles, between slaves and free men, between men and women; you are all one in union with Christ Jesus.' Those of us who are Christians need, as Catherina Halkes urges, to work for 'a qualitative transformation of the old existence [where] justice will play its part'.[7] This transformation will not take place overnight, nor will it eliminate all differences between men and women. Paul himself, in his letters to the young churches, still stresses the propriety of recognizing traditional styles of relationship. (In the appendix I outline some of the views, on 'headship' for example, which Christians draw from these texts.) At the same time, Paul accepts and reinforces the new place women are to occupy in kingdom work. Women were teachers, administrators and prophets in the early Church. Phoebe, entrusted with the letter to the Romans, is spoken of as a deacon (Romans 16). Priscilla's ministry was clearly acknowledged and reinforced by Paul, who sent the learned Apollos to her to learn more. We know that Philip's four daughters were all prophets and that many women played an important part in housing the local church in their homes. Chloë, Apphia and Priscilla again are all spoken of in this context. Many women are referred to by name as 'fellow-workers' in the gospel, a term also applied to Paul, Timothy, Titus, Luke and other men. Priscilla (Romans 16.3, Acts 18.18), Euodias and Syntyche (Philippians 4.2—3) are mentioned in this respect. Of the twenty-nine people greeted at the end of Romans 16, ten are women. Women indeed played a full part in the New Testament Church. Some of them also had an active life supporting themselves and others: Lydia (Acts 16.14—15), Dorcas (Acts 9.36—42) and Priscilla (Acts 18.24—6). Furthermore, in spite of what many might feel were Paul's teachings on 'headship', it is clear that Aquila and Priscilla did not exhibit a hierarchical marriage relationship, but Paul himself regarded the ministries of each on the same level.

There is evidence here then of the new dynamic that comes for women when we recognize that in Christ sin is conquered and a new freedom is possible. However, for a fuller model of that redemption life we need to turn to Jesus himself, and to his own relationships and attitudes to women.

Jesus and women

Many feminists who have found it difficult to identify with the maleness of God as so often portrayed by the Church, discover in the Jesus of the Gospels a person whom they love and appreciate. For what is so striking about Christ is that he *does not* uphold the male establishment. In all his attitudes and concern he rejects the patriarchal power structure of his day. He came into a society which, although it greatly improved on pagan societies, still held women in very low esteem. A woman was a minor all her life, she could only be divorced at her husband's request. Her legal position was inferior. She was not taught the Torah along with her brothers. She could not pass through the gentile porch in Herod's temple. As a reminder of Eve's tempting Adam into sin, a man was forbidden to be alone with a woman unless they were married. He was forbidden to look at a married woman. Jewish religious leaders would be defiled by looking on a woman, and their piety in this respect meant many injuries as they could not look up for fear of seeing the forbidden object.

Women, lepers, Samaritans, prostitutes, tax-gatherers were all the scum of respectable, religious Jewish society. Yet they were the very people who are recorded as being with Jesus and accepted by Jesus. Christ surprised even his own disciples, when for example he was alone with the Samaritan woman at the well. He surprised her too by asking for a drink, and thus making himself ritually unclean: he nevertheless revealed himself to her as the Messiah (John 4. 7−42). He had no words of condemnation for the woman taken in adultery, but prevented her death, telling her simply to sin no more (John 8.3−11). No reproach again was given to the woman with the haemorrhage, who by touching his cloak had both received healing yet 'defiled' him. She knew what she had done, and fear of the law rather than 'feminine modesty' made her reluctant to own up. Yet Christ commended her faith, implicitly dismissing the rigid Jewish taboos as irrelevant. The scandal caused because Christ accepted the love, kisses, tears and warmth of affection from a woman who was prepared to 'shame' herself by letting down her hair to wipe his feet brought only reproach to the men. Why were they not able to offer him the same physical love and care (Luke 7)? Her reputation did not matter: 'for she loved much', and had been forgiven everything.

Jesus not only accepted love from women, he accepted their financial provision for him too (Luke 8). He cut across his culture's stereotyping of women as seducers or fools, and treated them always with dignity. It was the woman who listened and learned that he commended, rather than the one who fulfilled the normal Jewish domestic role (Luke 10. 38−42). It was to a woman that he first disclosed himself as the Messiah; to a woman that he revealed himself as the

'Resurrection and the Life' (John 11.24–7); and from the same woman that he received the wholehearted affirmation: 'Yes, Lord; I believe that you are the Christ, the Son of God.'

He showed his gentleness with mothers who wanted to bring their children to him, and could not get past his disciples (Mark 10.13–15). He showed his love for the woman crippled for many years by touching her and healing her (Luke 13.10). He showed his concern for the widow, who was especially vulnerable. It was a poor widow whose generosity he singled out for praise, and a widow's son whom he raised and restored to his mother (Luke 21.3; 7.11–17). His thoughts whilst in great pain on the cross were for his own mother, for one to take his place as her son and bring her comfort.

Jesus never 'condescended' to women, and never ignored them. His message was to them as much as to the men. As the Christ, the Son of God, he was representative of the whole human race. He came as human (*anthropos*), not as man (*aner*). He had come to seek and to save those who were lost. It was important that his teachings reached women as well as men, and to this end he rejected the formal and very 'masculine' teaching of his day, and spoke in homely, everyday terms. He used illustrations which would speak to women: yeast and bread, grinding corn, looking for lost coins, sewing new cloth on old garments, wedding feasts, the persistent widow. His unpatronizing attitude communicated respect and dignity and brought him their love.

The harsh words he spoke were never for women: they were for the powerful male establishment. It was the religious leaders whom he called whitewashed tombs and accused of hypocrisy, it was a political leader he denounced as a 'fox', it was greedy businessmen whom he called 'thieves'.

Here, then, was no male-dominant model. His message was that his followers were not to 'lord it over' others but that 'whoever wants to become great among you must be your servant, and whoever wants to be first must be your slave'. What is more his words had power, for this is how he lived: 'just as the Son of Man did not come to be served, but to serve and give his life a ransom for many' (Matthew 20.25–8). Small wonder that the women loved him so much. Small wonder that after one of his disciples had betrayed him and another denied him the women were prepared to risk everything for his sake. The women were there at the foot of the cross. The women were there to anoint his body on the third day. And the women were there to see the stone rolled away, the empty tomb, and the reality of resurrection. He was the one they knew him to be: the Redeemer, the Messiah, and for us as for them he has brought liberation.

Notes

1. See, for example, Mary Evans *Woman in the Bible.* (Paternoster Press 1983); P. DeJong and D. Wilson *Husband and Wife* (Zondervan 1979); Shirley Lees (ed.) *The Role of Women When Christians Disagree* in the Inter-varsity Press 1984; James Hurley *Man and Woman in Biblical Perspective.* Inter-varsity Press 1981; Letha Scanzoni and Nancy Hardesty, *All We're Meant to Be.* (Word Books 1974).
2. Don Wilson, 'A Biblical Critique of Traditional Sex Roles' in *Husband and Wife,* p. 123.
3. See appendix on 'Headship'.
4. Martin Luther, *Commentary on Genesis* (Zondervan 1958), p. 82.
5. Helmuth Thielicke (trans. John W. Doberstein) *The Ethics of Sex* (Harper and Row 1964), p. 8.
6. P. DeJong and D. Wilson, *Husband and Wife* (Zondervan 1979), p. 136.
7. Jane Burns, 'Feminism in the Church' *(Catholic Herald* 30 November 1984).

14: Christian Feminism Today

Two questions have been implicit throughout the whole book. Should Christians be involved in feminism, and what would such a feminism look like today? In this last chapter I want to draw together answers to these questions.

Feminism is a response to structural questions which will not go away. There is widespread injustice to women in our society. The same issue crops up in family life, education, the law, the Church and marriage: women are not respected as men's equals. They are frequently used and abused. Many women in fact experience not only frustration and discrimination but also real oppression at the hands of some men.

One answer is nevertheless to counsel against any involvement in feminism on the grounds that, as Christians create the right climate, these problems will be sorted out without intervention. One could argue that feminism in fact exacerbates the issue and makes women worse off. It is better to allow and encourage society to develop in such a way that justice will surface and the position of women will improve. I believe that, like most *laissez-faire* responses, this is unrealistic. To start with, 'creating the right climate' is a very active (and often interventionist) endeavour. But the situation is that the problems are getting worse. As we saw in the first part of the book, in some areas women are now shown less respect and concern, and differences between the sexes are more emphatic, than they were some years ago. This is symptomatic of a widespread social deterioration. In our post-Christian culture norms of truth, care, mutual responsibility, trust and faithfulness are uncomfortably absent. Permanent unemployment, people as commodities, increasing violence, women depersonalized as sex aids, breakdown of marital trust and more emphasis on power do not justify any optimism about society's evolutionary improvement. Nor can Christians assume that this is merely an 'external' problem, scratching at the door. Like any other kind of sin, it is also inside the Christian community, in the cupboards, the bedrooms and even swept under the carpet. The hope that Christians can just 'create the right climate' is dangerously complacent.

Another answer is to say that these problems can be met on an individual level. Marriage guidance counsellors should be available to help a woman with a 'husband problem'. School teachers should keep an eye open for early male chauvinism in the classroom. Women should not work for bosses who treat them with no respect. More women ought to stand for parliament to strengthen the female presence there. Yet, although these measures might tackle immediate issues, the problem is clearly much bigger than this. For the patriarchal emphasis of our society means that the unjust way many men behave towards women is legitimated in legal and economic structures. It is embedded in attitudes and stereotypes. Those women who object to all of this are frequently pilloried; their womanliness is challenged because they will not have it defined for them by a male-dominated culture. An individual response then can only work away at small areas. The problem is also an overall structural one, and as such needs a coherent structural response.

Yet the particular structural responses we have examined in this book objectify the problem in ways that at best are only partial and at worst wrongly based. For example, whilst it is very important to recognize with the Marxists the capitalist use of women, at home or at work, that is only one form of disrespect. The male antipathy that the radical feminists identify is also less of an explanation than is sometimes suggested, for men also exploit men. Both these positions offer much help in analysing the basic issues yet, because they start from the view of human autonomy, both fall into the trap of making the problem total. A still bigger danger is that they move into a position of self-righteousness. The fault is always external: man, patriarchy, capitalism, the class structure. There are always two camps and the problem is necessarily with the other camp. This self-righteous stance can easily distance women from the possibility of self-critical attitudes. To have my consciousness raised to my oppression must go hand in hand with raising my consciousness to my sin. The debate needs to be lifted out of these polarizations.

So there is a need for Christians to be involved in these issues specifically as *Christian* feminists, recognizing at the same time that 'a Christian witness which addresses itself to a redirection of society may never be restricted to personal testimonies and individual lifestyle.'[1] Sin which grips people's lives in a thousand different ways has become institution-alized into social structures and behavioural patterns which have distorted and perverted the truth. Whilst recognizing some of the surface problems and their growth historically we also need to see what we are up against in putting it right. People, groups, societies, ruling élites have committed themselves to their idols, whether these be economic growth, company profits, power, personal affluence, professional status or an indulgent sexual life. And such idols are greedy for worship and not easily satisfied. For many people this worship is total. Their lives are now lived within a framework which precludes any deep analysis of what might be wrong; they are unable to understand those who live outside their framework. Some people will not be able to read this book because they no longer accept the categories for understanding what I have been saying. Basic concepts such as justice and fairness have been redefined by them to fit into a certain political and economic package. It is not simply that they are insensitive and unable to sympathize with those who suffer. It is that worship of their idol blinds them to the possibility of such awareness. They live in a differently defined 'reality'. It is a fight in the end against principalities and powers and calls for a common Christian response.

A Christian feminist analysis

Initially for Christian feminists as for others the issue is the same. *Men* constitute a problem for women, not as individuals necessarily, but as those who combine to impose certain attitudes and values, to uphold certain interests in society. Pay differentials, educational priorities, rape, domestic violence, pornography, workloads in the home, leisure patterns all produce their own evidence to indicate the extent of the problem. For it is woven into the very structure of contemporary society. Big careers for men are massaged by multinational corporations, professional bodies, employment agencies and the Civil Service. The links of the establishment pass through schools, clubs and associations which are exclusively male. The Church is so often identified as an infallible male élite. Modern marriage can easily be seen as a pattern of convenience which especially suits men. Male attitudes combine with male structures and reinforce the superiority of men. Aggression, pride, self-glorification and selfishness often cohere in the way men treat women. Many women spend their lives 'humouring' the men they live with or work with in order to minimize disharmony. It is understandable that some women want to escape from all this and espouse a woman-centred life-style.

The Christian feminist will not go that way however. For although it may prove hard to convince some men of this, a Christian feminism will not be trying to polarize the sexes. It has a different starting-point. For the root issue is not patriarchy, or even patriarchy-plus-capitalist-exploitation. These themselves are only symptoms of a deeper problem still. The sin that takes its root in the human heart feeds into human and social structures and perverts and distorts relationships. I find it interesting that even though Christians are often accused of having a pessimistic view of human nature with its accent on sin, this view actually emerges as much more optimistic than the others we have looked at. For many radical feminists discussed in this book have simply had to write men off. Men produce patriarchy, and patriarchy is beyond redemption. Yet unlike these non-Christian feminists, many of whom have been hurt beyond the point where they can see any future in relationships with men, Christian women can recognize always the possibility of change and reconciliation. Repentance is a real alternative.

The liberation of men
One crucial feature of the stance we are adopting here is that Christian feminism is committed not just to the liberation of women, but to the liberation of men also. What is more, this liberation is not only from class oppression, from work alienation, but from the very slavery that a sin-ridden, male-dominated culture has produced. For cultural stereotypes have prevented men too from knowing real freedom. Men in the Church have been stunted in their growth towards Christian maturity, as they are unable to experience the blessings which follow from being emptied of self and naked in one's vulnerability. Many Christian men throughout Britain and the United States still think it unmanly to weep, to show remorse, to express emotion in a way which will be noticed.

163

So many men feel the need to distance themselves as far as possible from their feelings. In our rationalistic, cerebral age a display of feelings is either theatrical, indulgent or indicates a person is out of control. The only feelings men are allowed to exhibit are ones of anger, irritation or impatience.

It is not surprising then that embedded in many marital problems is a husband's inability to show affection and share himself in a deep and personal way. He may also see his marriage as secondary to work or leisure, and not be used to investing time and energy in it. Women, socialized since childhood into making friendships and frequently meeting other women on a more familiar and personal level, often find marriage dissatisfying because the relationship stays superficial, and basic needs of companionship, warmth, sharing and affection are not met. Although many men feel they show their affection through sex, women who are wanting an intimate relationship of a broader and deeper kind see sexual affection on its own as shallow. But it is not only with women that men are crippled by the stereotypes which have been developed in them. Relationships between men often deteriorate into competitiveness and assertion, where pride dominates, and no one dares to admit being wrong or making a mistake. Patriarchal values of dominance and power-seeking have their grips on men, whether at work, driving a car, or in the home, and enslave them as much as women. The growth of men's groups where men can relax together and try to verbalize their feelings of frustration, happiness, sorrow or being let down testifies how many men themselves are concerned to escape from the rigid male roles prescribed. The difficulty some of them experience initially in such groups betrays the tenacity with which these attitudes are held.

Christian feminists are not therefore wanting any power struggle with men. That would be entirely foreign to their agenda. Nor are they wanting to construct an all-female reality which washes its hands of any involvement with the other sex. But they are not happy simply to slip into a slot marked 'woman' and live their lives according to a set of prescribed cultural and essentially non-biblical values. The message they bring is a message of liberation, and it is for men also.

So what, more comprehensively, does this liberation mean?

It does not mean freedom to do what one wants, or even independence from the other sex. The lie of Enlightenment autonomy is finally repudiated both for men and for women. The root Christian view of liberation is of freedom from sin before God, and sin with all the ramifications already outlined. Surprisingly, this opens up the way to follow what has been described, albeit superficially, as womanly values. Forgiven men and women are free to pursue gentleness, patience, peace, longsuffering, self-control in their relationships with one another. Forgiveness brings restoration and healing. The apostle Paul, so often caricatured as a male chauvinist, made these attitudes the core of all Christian relationships. The choice is therefore between the selfishness and self-glorification of the old sexual stereotypes and the commitment of faith to the costly way which Christ outlined and fulfilled. The great enigma is that the grace necessary for this can only be given by God and cannot be demanded.

Some broader implications
This outline of some Christian feminist principles can be developed more when we look again at a few of the areas which concerned the secular feminists in part one of the book. So often we will stand together on our critique. When we look at pornography we will all see the distortion of women, the exploitation of the female body for male greed and lust, and the depersonalization of both men and women that results. When we look at popular literature we will together see magazines which harm girls at a vulnerable adolescent stage, with an emphasis on appearances, on the kind of relationships with boys and role expectations which already limit the possibilities for their growing into maturity. When we look at education we will be able to see the reinforcement of certain behaviour patterns and the verbal segregation of boys' and girls' abilities. But the meaning and explanation we give to what we see will be different, and very often so will be our way forward.

To illustrate this I want to focus on the two issues which opened the book: work and family relationships. What might a Christian feminist have to say specifically in these areas which differs from the analysis of non-feminists and non-Christians?

Work

One thing here is certain: a Christian feminist would not only be working for women's rights in the workplace. Yet she would be doing at least that. For clearly these are important, since as we saw, women are particularly powerless in this area. Injustice is still structured into the very definition of many women's jobs. It is unjust that women who work long hours in demanding jobs should be paid less than men. It is unjust that women with equal training and skill should stay at the bottom rungs of the professional ladder whilst men climb to the top. Sexism in the sphere of work is very evident and it is wrong. It is wrong in attitudes of employers, of colleagues, of the workforce, of the unions and of the legislators. What is more, like inequality in general, it affects the most vulnerable women worst of all. But sexual inequality and sexist attitudes are only part of what is wrong in the area of work today, and it is important for the Christian feminist to address the question in its wider context. What is needed is something much bigger than changes in law, or better education. The very *meaning* of work is at stake.

Work is an essential part of all our lives. It is mentioned in the account of creation: it is part of what men and *women* were made for. For Christians particularly (though not exclusively) work is the way we express both our dependence on the rest of creation and our responsibility as its stewards. Work, not idleness, is the Christian norm. This does not mean of course that work has to be defined in monetary terms, nor that anyone who is not working for remuneration needs to be regarded as idle. This present system of evaluating work is harmful, where status, privileges, prestige and power are attached to some forms of work and not others. It is all the more questionable since this is often for reasons little to do with the actual work itself. Housework and childcare are just as much work as mining or engineering. Care of an elderly partner or relative is just as much work as retailing or professional sport. Counselling at a rape crisis centre is just as much work as judging a beauty competition. The present structure of work which elevates some, whilst making other kinds of workers (usually women) economically dependent on charity or 'handouts' ought to be substantially revised. The community's responsibility for payment for such work is already recognized in the area of child and adult fostering, but there are many other tasks which are downgraded in public valuation. Christian feminist research might well examine ways in which systems of payment could properly remunerate women's work and make their economic position less vulnerable. The deeper issue, however, is the way in which the meaning of women's work, whether in the office, factory or home, needs to be honoured and respected. Women's time matters as much as men's. Reasonable pay and job satisfaction should not be male prerogatives.

When we look at other aspects of a Christian doctrine of work it is evident that the work enterprise is to be structured by norms. Stewardship, service, co-operation, creativity and justice are all evident in biblical teaching,[2] yet are uncomfortably absent in contemporary ideologies and practices. We can see this dissonance clearly in the areas of *creativity*. In the Christian framework work should be an expression of who we are, of our very selves in all our difference, individuality and createdness. Yet much work today is far from being creative or human; it is more frequently humdrum and monotonous, with people used like tools. Edward Vanderkloet summarizes the problems which arise when this takes place.

Work should provide us with a profound sense of satisfaction; it should give us a sense of self-fulfilment. For a factory not only shapes products, it shapes people . . . It is therefore deeply tragic that countless workers in our society are deprived of the satisfaction of accomplishment due to the nature and structure of their work. Such people are virtually forced to seek happiness in leisure and the possession of goods.[3]

This alienation is a very real experience for women as well as men. It means that many women spend the months counting down to the next holiday. Some women even look to childbirth as a way of 'escape'. Justifying the low worth given to women's employment is the deeply-held assumption that women's 'creativity' belongs only in the home. Yet, as we have seen, even this creativity is not honoured in the economy as a whole. But at the end of it all the norm of creative work remains as the standard by which women's jobs are to be evaluated.

When we turn to the norms of *co-operation* and *service* a similar pattern is all too evident. Lack of job satisfaction, anger and resentment at the often unreasonable inequalities of employment, have produced a deep-seated polarization, to the extent that competition and confrontation rather than co-operation rule so much of the work environment. Those with economic and political power who are in a position to dictate the terms of another's work often try to force their will on the workforce. Male workers often resist demands for equality from women workers, feeling them to be a threat. Firms faced with changes in the law will reclassify jobs artificially rather than give justice to women. Confrontation is now structured into our western capitalist system. The labour unions have certainly played a vital part in safeguarding the conditions under which people are employed but in another sense they have erected another force—the force of the collective—over against the power of institutionalized individualism and self-interest. Time and again we have witnessed industrial deadlock where neither side is committed to justice and where the more powerful wins. Sometimes this reaches a relaxed truce where each side learns to live with and respect the other, but at other times the emergence of a powerful interventionist government, especially of the New Right, can make the struggle a very uneven one. Caught up in these tension are ordinary women *whose work matters* because it is part of their humanity, part of what it is to be made in the image of God. Yet so often they are treated as though it does not matter. The message which comes over to them with unmistakable clarity from those with vested interests is that profits matter more than people. Our contemporary capitalist work ethic is happy to sacrifice them on the altar of mammon.

Like creativity, service and co-operation, *stewardship* and *justice* have departed from the contemporary meaning of work, leaving a gap through which the wind blows on to many continents. For national self-interest is so much more important than economic justice to the Third World. Women in these countries suffer keenly and acutely, in ways we can only read about but never begin to experience. If sisterhood means anything then it means it here. Christian feminists who take justice in the work sphere seriously should be found amongst those facing the issues of women's illness and disease, takeover of their land, exclusion from trading, lack of education and other forms of women's deprivation in the

Third World. This is a challenge which makes domestic problems seem insignificant.

A Christian feminism then will not simply be interested in furthering the rights of a large number of middle-class professional women, or even simply fighting the issues of sexual discrimination. It will be concerned also to challenge the economic idols of society: growth, technology and progress, to which we all must bow. It will be especially concerned to call into question the very meaning and structure of work in contemporary society, and the way this structure confers power, but *leaves most women powerless.*

There will be several levels on which this task might be attempted. Careful analysis and research would necessarily precede any drawing up of policies for action. But there are organizations also which might be willing to take on board a Christian feminist agenda.[4] Women could also be ready to establish pressure groups of their own. A Christian women's trade union would not be out of the question, where feminists could seek to support actively women in many forms of work who are presently without much representation. Finally, on a more local and individual level, Christians could well set up work co-operatives in which stewardship, service, creativity, co-operation and justice would be exhibited. Here women would know the freedom of working in community and knowing respect and equality, and the joy of doing the task for which they might be well suited.

Being human in our work, then, will involve much restructuring in a society which would deny our humanness. It will also inevitably involve us in thinking through issues in many other areas. It is to one of these, the area of marriage and the family, that I now want to return.

Marriage and the family
Although with the issue of marriage we consider a different set of norms and patterns of relationships from those of work, the underlying point I am making is curiously identical. It is that marriage in our society has become robbed of its meaning. As they are lived today marriages are so often private, functional and indulgent. Within the marriage the wife is vulnerable and economically defensive; her identity has often become embedded in her domestic roles. The man

has traditionally had greater opportunities to form liaisons outside marriage, and although the dual standards of sexual morality may almost have gone, deceit and adultery are still seen as more prevalent among husbands than among wives. In spite of being one of the idols of modern society (or maybe because of it) marriage is in a mess. The humanist perspective has not liberated marriage but enslaved those who have followed it. For the desire for *self*-fulfilment, *self*-achievement, *self*-growth and *self*-service is what has produced chauvinism in men. For women to travel further down the same road can only make the situation worse. It will lead a thousand miles away from the biblical position of love, troth and mutual submission. A Christian feminist therefore recognizes the hollowness of contemporary forms of marriage, and would not rush to champion these against more trothful and committed relationships where no wedding has taken place. The secular feminist distaste for shallow and manipulative marriage relationships is understandable. For a Christian however, some of their alternatives are not acceptable.

To examine why this is so we need to return to our starting-point, and at the same time to draw together some of the threads scattered throughout the book. Marriage, the close and committed relationship between man and woman, was part of the creation account in the Old Testament. Woman and man were created as 'one flesh' and given the task of procreation. The New Testamant fills out the relationship: marriage is to be loving, faithful, respectful, trothful and patient. It is to be one in which the partners nourish and cherish each other. Wives are to respect their husbands and husbands are to honour and love their wives. This does not portray marriage as a haven or refuge from the rest of the world. It sees the relationship as a public one, woven into the work and worship of the Christian community, but one in which the 'marriage bed' is to be honoured. Marriage does not mean the end of friendships or physical affection outside marriage: the fact that it has often been interpreted this way leaves many single people feeling very isolated and lonely. Marriage does not mean that the husband or wife has to meet all the needs of the other partner. It does not entail ownership or possession. It does not rob a person of his or her individuality. But it does involve a very close and special bonding upheld by the 'one flesh' principle. It involves deep care and nourishment. It involves sexual exclusiveness: no adultery or unfaithfulness. It involves voluntary and deliberate commitment.

The emphasis which Paul places on the marriage relationship illustrates both his concern for the protection of women in a harshly male-dominated culture, and also the need for *love.* This love is not the romantic or fleeting variety. It is the patient, tender, self-controlling love which does not assert itself, is not vain and keeps no score of wrongs (1 Corinthians 13). It is also physical sexual love. This love is to be the bedrock of life together. He chooses two examples of how a man should love his wife (Ephesians 5). One is that he should love his wife as he loves his own body. This homely example presents a tall order. The detailed daily care we lavish on our bodies to keep them fed, healthy, comfortable, warm, nourished, free from pain and in good shape is a high priority in most of our lives. We have to look after our bodies. If we neglect this care we know we shall suffer. This same detailed nourishment is the picture of love within marriage. The second analogy is that a man should love his wife as Christ loves the Church. The self-denying, sacrificial love which listens and understands, puts the other first and gives up its very life in service should go alongside the detailed daily cherishing of the earlier example. It is interesting that this is the love *husbands* are instructed to give. It is probably because Paul recognized that men then, as well as now, were the ones who could use this advice. It seems to me that if this kind of love were evident in marriage today far fewer feminists would be looking for alternatives!

What is interesting also about the biblical references to marriage (and to family life too) is that they leave a great deal of space for differences. There are no rigidly prescribed roles, no specified division of labour within the family, no stereotypic notions of what it is to be a manly husband or a good housewife. (The most famous housewife in the Bible, the woman in Proverbs 31, was a long call from our watered-down, distorted, modern 'Christian' ideal.) These, then, are all cultural ideas which we have loaded into marriage and the family, and it is the gripping power of these which destroys Christian creativity. In the Scriptures the mother is not given the task of rearing children: the responsibility is specifically that of both parents. Wherever instruction is given to children on family duties, it is responsibility to both parents which is stressed. When fathers are singled out it is to be told not to provoke the children, not to discourage them (Ephesians 6; Colossians 3). What is clear then is that the scope for different role patterns, different task assignments within the home is very wide. The traditional male breadwinner/domestic wife is not sealed with an indelible scriptural stamp. It is one of the options open. But so are many others. Jointly shared working and domestic roles are equally Christian. So is the situation where the man cares for the family, and the wife earns their income. So is the sharing of child care among a number of families or within the extended family. What has produced the pattern which now exists are the demands of a male-oriented career pattern, outside economic interests and the structure of work, not the biblical understanding of marriage and the family. Fathers who have postponed their careers in order to be around near their children at a crucial stage in their lives, mothers who have found a use for their skills outside as well as inside the home, have often been enriched as parents and people as well as married partners

Christian freedom implies being free to serve, and free to break from a mould into which we do not easily fit. For many this will not imply anything very radical. It may well be that the majority of women are happiest to be at home in a traditional role, especially whilst children are small. They should not be despised for this or made to feel less than a person. But this should not be elevated either as the Christian norm for all women. Families themselves should be left free to discover their own way of loving, caring, nurturing and supporting each member so that all grow into full personhood.

There is one important note about the relation between family and work which has not yet been sounded. It will not be easy to break away from traditional patterns. A woman who moves out of work to have and stay with children has always been the one penalized in the present work structure. If a man chooses to 'give' his wife more freedom by not being prepared to move with his firm, by standing out against Sunday and overtime work, or by taking on a substantial proportion of domestic responsibilities, it will mean a sacrifice for him in career terms. If he moves on to a part-time job he will suffer not only a drop in salary, but all promotion chances will be lowered, status and privileges will be reduced, and he will be given a distinct label. Our capitalist, competitive work structure is a very demanding taskmaster and ensures that those who deviate from the norm are not going to hold any influence in the way the rest of the system develops. There is always a price to be paid.

Abortion

Because the issue of abortion has been one of the planks of the modern feminist movement, this section must also address this issue. For a Christian feminist the question is a complex one. On the one hand 'sister' feminists see abortion on demand as one of the basic steps to woman's freedom, and this view has not changed even when feminists have been concerned to rediscover and recapture the importance of mothering. Even Germaine Greer's sensitive *Sex and Destiny,* regarded by many as a massive departure from her earlier writings, still endorses the necessity of abortion: 'Abortion is not a stop-gap between here and some future perfect contraceptive; it can very well be the chosen method of birth control for more and more women . . . rather than lamenting that choice, the sensible course of action would seem to be to provide the best possible abortion service.'[5] On the other hand, 'fellow' Christians have traditionally been anti-abortionists, focusing not so much on the freedom of women, but on the sanctity of human life. The fact that anti-abortion campaigns often ride with a militant anti-feminism makes it even more difficult for a Christian feminism to affirm its stand on the issue.

The starting-point seems fundamental. The argument for easy abortion always depends on the view of the human embryo as something less than human, as initially simply an extension of the woman's own bodily tissue, and later as something formed but still not human. In that case who can deny the woman's right to choose what to do with her own body? However, those of us who find difficulty with this view of the embryo cannot accept that it is a question of the mother's (or her parents', husband's or boyfriend's) 'choice'. If from the beginning another human personality is involved, another independent life is at stake, the question of 'whose choice?' becomes a very doubtful one. Whilst we have to recognize the agony brought on many women by unwanted pregnancies, the solution to this agony cannot surely be to legalize the destruction of another growing human personality.

But this is no glib statement. For if we are to make such a stand against the present looseness of the abortion laws we need also to take full responsibility for the effects of any changes or repeal. We also need to get away from the harshness which stereotypes all women who present themselves for abortion, and recognize the hardships and suffering which drive many women to take this step. John Stott summarizes well the Christian responsibility towards changing the law: 'To agitate for it without being prepared to bear its cost would be sheer hypocrisy.'[6]

Compassion and practical help on a personal level must go alongside a social and educational programme which ensures that women would not become more vulnerable. What is more, *radical* changes on men's parts are necessary if any viable alternative is to be worked through. These changes will have to start with the Christian community. If men are really to love their wives, share their children's lives, respect their sisters and honour all women, they will need to turn their backs on some of the strongest male values in our culture. In many cases they will need to forge a new Christian identity, and set a new trend in compassion which might begin to redirect images of manliness in our culture. If abortion on demand is to be opposed on Christian grounds — and it is — then we have to ensure that women are not left weaker and more vulnerable as a result.

Singleness

Other than on the issue of abortion, most of this section has focused on what a Christian feminism looks like in relation to marriage and the family. However, many women are not married and have no children. We have already indicated how isolating this can be. How does a Christian feminism address those who are single, therefore? What does it have to say about singleness to the Christian community as a whole? Perhaps just two basic points ought to be made in this chapter. Single women are not failures, and single women have needs.

The attitudes to single Christian women in particular which see them as unfulfilled and unsuccessful because marriage has eluded them are harmful both for women themselves and for the community as a whole. Studies done comparing single with married women today show they are less likely to suffer nervous breakdowns, they have fewer emotional problems, and they are physically healthier.[7] Many Christian women have chosen a single life, not to escape marital responsibility, but because they have felt it necessary in order to serve God. Nancy Hardesty writes: 'It is sadly ironic that the Protestant church in its revolt against mediaeval monasticism elevates marriage and denigrates celibacy, and yet almost requires singleness of women who wish to serve the church. Many women, however, do love God and want to serve him enough to make this sacrifice.'[8] Other women are single because, simply, they have not found anyone they wish to marry. Many are single because the demands of a professional job have not been those they could reconcile with married and family life in the social climate they live in. However, because marriage is such a strong cultural idol, we feel those who are still single by the age of thirty ought to account for themselves, otherwise we shall label them as failures.

Because marriage and motherhood have been so widely identified as woman's true vocation, single women are often seen as only half-women, and as such they have been assumed not to have the same human needs as the married population. Yet needs of love, warmth, companionship, comfort, care and touch are important to all of us. Radical feminists have been aware of this for a decade, and have provided a focus for these needs in their lives together. Sisterhood has brought the warmth, love, recognition and self-affirmation which the male-dominated society has denied. Sadly, the Church has still to learn this, and to put its love into practice. Fears of being misunderstood mean that unmarried women are often not shown physical affection. But hugging, touching, stroking need not have sexual overtones. They should be a spontaneous way of sharing our love for one another.

A more problematic issue for single women is coming to terms with sexual feelings. Since sex screams at us from every avenue in society, sexual arousal can often come unawares and present real problems. People are grossly manipulated today, in the hope of stimulating sex for further ends: usually to sell something. In a climate where chastity is outmoded and virginity is a joke, the single Christian woman can find sexual loneliness to be acute. Casual sexual encounters, relationships outside marriage, are not for her, and she has to face temptations unsupported by Christian friends because she often cannot confide her feelings. Again, understanding and supportiveness rather than distance and stereotyping would make a great deal of difference.

One issue we have not discussed is that of lesbianism. Although there is much debate on this my own belief is that a practising lesbianism is not a Christian option. The biblical teaching links sexual intercourse so much with the 'one flesh' principle between a woman and a man, and places great restraint on homosexual practices. It is true, too, that widespread promiscuity is so often a feature of homosexuality. At the same time, we have to be aware that many lesbian relationships are closer to the norms of troth, commitment, love and faithfulness than many hetereosexual marriages, and not ignore this. What is more, Christians again have been slow to show understanding to homosexuals at times of grief and bereavement, and have been very ready to condemn. What is clearly needed much more is sensitive Christian counselling for adolescents at a time when they are forming a sexual identity. The range of feelings and emctions which we all have is very broad, and alongside committed radical lesbians many girls (and boys) turn to homosexuality because they have lacked encouragement, support and affirmation at a crucial stage of their lives.

Conclusion

Although there has been space to focus on only a few areas, a Christian feminism has broader implications than addressing issues of work, marriage, family and singleness. For injustice to women is not rooted in one sphere but is present in every aspect of life: sexual, historical, linguistic, social, economic, legal, aesthetic and ecclesiastical. A Christian feminist perspective needs therefore to be developed in each area, and an agenda put forward for initiating research and directives in each sphere. In the areas of literature and education, concerns very different from those in marriage or work would bring a different set of issues to consider. Useful research could be done into teaching methods, into school curricula, into school reading materials which would begin to redress the assumption of male supremacy. But it would be done too in the context of our creatureliness rather than our independence and autonomy, and would need to go hand in hand with respect for each other and for the rest of creation. The way we learn and the assumptions presently made about the way we learn is another whole area which other feminists are also investigating, and which would form part of our agenda. Some of the excellent and very basic booklets on issues as fundamental as learning in groups[9] would, if put into practice, implement some important Christian feminist ideas. The whole education system as it now exists must come under review: the 'two worlds' of independent and state education in Britain, and the mushrooming system of Christian education in America. What does Christian education mean? What is a Christian school? We have to be careful not simply to endorse a school which espouses the American dream of success, and perpetuates male chauvinism, values of affluence, individualism and scientism just because it calls itself Christian. Real Christian education will be something deeper and something which will be essentially *critical* of the assumptions of the day, however much they may be part of our culture.

A Christian feminist agenda has still more to consider than education. There is a need for Christian women's literature which goes beyond stereotypes and enters into real dialogue with women. Girls' and women's magazines, novels and short stories could in themselves open up new avenues. Christian women could be encouraged to write themselves, seeing their own insights and experiences as valuable enough to share with others and so building up a new feminine awareness. There are plays, poems and biographies waiting to be written, songs to be composed, dances to be choreographed. Christian women have dabbled on the very edges of corporate creativity in the arts. Because we have experienced our femininity as restricting rather than liberating we have not claimed the land which is our birthright. We do not need to ape secular culture or male dominated art forms. We live in God's world and it is ours to experience, enjoy and experiment with. Literature, song, painting and dance can be indeed used as our celebration of humanness and womanhood.

Another aspect of feminist research in the aesthetic sphere would be to focus on notions of feminine beauty, propagated by women's magazines and endorsed too by so many Christian publications. Basically we are witnessing the dominance of male definitions of beauty, seen in terms of sexual attractiveness and youthfulness. It seems important fundamentally to challenge these views of attractiveness and the way the superficiality of these concepts inflicts a distorted perception of their own beauty on women themselves. It is also big business, and many women are gripped by the obsession to look young: to wear cosmetic masks to hide physical 'defects' because they cannot face themselves as they are. Christian feminism would want to open up much deeper understanding and free women from these cords.

When we turn to the ecclesiastical sphere we might want to reappraise the accepted norm of leadership patterns, looking more at sharing skills and less at a one-person ministry. Apart from bringing women more responsibility and less frustration, this would open up the whole lay participation of the Church, and move away from a professional élite. The whole professional monopoly everywhere in society would need to be reconsidered, for not only does it strengthen male dominance, but it so often penalizes the weak and uninformed. Measures limiting the powers and privileges of the professions and making them more accountable to a public which includes women may well require the activity of professional women themselves who are able to move away from self-interest into a deeper desire to see justice and fairness prevail.

A Christian feminist programme would clearly be no piece of cake. Nor would it be the indulgent self-seeking which in many people's minds often epitomizes feminism today. Throughout it all the underlying critique is of contemporary humanism, and *a humanism in which men define the norms.* Instead the desire is to recover a Christian definition: to discern how women are to be treated in God's terms and to move our society from being one which debases and devalues them to one in which they have dignity, equality, and freedom to be really human. God created people as male and female, and this difference will always be there. What need not be there are the penalties women pay for their sex in so many areas of life. Following the tradition from which they come Christian feminists will not be working and praying on their own account and from their own self-concerns, but to really help those to liberation who need it most. The programme might be a daunting one. But the alternatives are less than human.

Notes

1. Ed Vanderkloet, 'Why Work Anyway?' in P. Marshall *et al*, *Labour of Love* (Wedge Publications 1980), p. 44.
2. Gen. 1.26–31, 2.15; Ps. 24.1; Prov. 23.4; Eccles. 2.24; Isa. 5.8; Amos 4.1–2, 8.4–7; Matt. 25.31–46; Luke 14.12–14; 1 John 3.17–18.
3. 'Why Work Anyway?' p. 39.
4. For example, the Committee for Justice and Liberty in Washington, the trade union the Christian Labour Association of Canada and the British 'Jubilee Centre' in Cambridge are all working in the areas of economic justice from a specifically Christian standpoint.
5. Germaine Greer, *Sex and Destiny: The Politics of Human Fertility* (Secker and Warburg 1984), p. 196.
6. John Stott, *Issues Facing Christians Today* (Marshall, Morgan and Scott 1984), p. 297.
7. J. Bernard, *The Future of Marriage: His and Hers* (World Publications 1972), pp. 29–30.
8. Letha Scanzoni and Nancy Hardesty, *All We're Meant To Be* (Word Books 1974), p. 148.
9. See, for example, the booklets produced by Scripture Union on leading group sessions.

Appendix

Headship and submission

Some of the differences of view occur because translating the Greek word for head, *kephalē,* into an exact contemporary English equivalent is by no means straightforward. For the word itself is used in many different ways in the New Testament. The literal, common usage signifies the physical 'head' (Matthew 10.30, Mark 15.19, Luke 7.46). The same word, *kephalē,* is used in 1 Peter 2. 19 and Matthew 21. 42 to refer to Christ as the cornerstone, the 'head of the corner'. Then Christ is spoken of as the 'head of the body'—the Church—in Ephesians 1.22, 4.15 and 5.23, although in 1 Corinthians 12.12—25 the 'body' is used in a different context, incorporating members of the Church into parts of the 'head'—ears and eyes. Men are spoken of as 'head' in relation to their wives in Ephesians 5, and it is the principle of 'headship' as gleaned from this passage, and the very difficult passage of 1 Corinthians 11, which focuses the debate today. What does this 'headship' entail? Is it one of authority in the way that *kephalē* seemed to represent Christ's authority over the Church? Colossians 1.18, 2.10 and 2.19 would throw doubt on that understanding of the Greek. For the word 'head' is used here not in terms of Christ's *authority* over the body, but in terms of Christ as the *source* or *origin* of the body. He is 'before all things and in him all things hold together'. Christ is 'the head of the body, the church, the beginning and the first born from the dead'. The point that 'head' most likely means 'source' here comes out even more strongly in Colossians 2 where we read that Christ is the head of all power and authority. So there references to 'head' convey the frequent metaphorical use of *kephalē* as beginning, origin or source. It can sometimes also be read as meaning 'goal' or 'aim'.

Some of the positions we will look at accept and incorporate this idea of head into their understanding of headship. Others retain the emphasis on authority and therefore hold a different view. I will outline briefly each of them in turn.

a) The first view sees 'headship' as the defining characteristic of all relationships between men and women. It was laid down in the very creation (1 Timothy 2.13) and in the order in which men and women were made. The divine hierarchy is Christ — man — woman. Thus just as man takes his authority from Christ and is to submit to him, so woman is under the authority of man, and is to submit. Men are women's 'heads' in the Church, in public office, in business and family life. Headship is about having authority and making decisions and exercising discipline. For a woman to enter into an authoritative office in the Church particularly would be sinful (1 Timothy 2). Women are essentially domestic and their proper sphere is that of subordinate 'helpmeet'. Women were created from men and for men and not the other way round (1 Corinthians 11).

b) The second view sees headship as limited to just two institutions. Even though the *order* of creation might seem to imply that men are to have general authority over women, in fact the passages in the New Testament dealing with headship deal with it only in terms of marriage and the Church. A woman is to be subordinate to the (male) headship of elders in the Church (1 Corinthians 14, 1 Timothy 2), and is to have no position of authority. Similarly she is to be submissive to the headship of her husband in marriage (Ephesians 5, Colossians 3, Titus 2. 5). The authority structure between husband and wife is like that between Christ and the Church, which means that authority must be exercised in love and care, not in self-assertion and dominance. Beyond marriage and the Church women may freely exercise authority over men — for example in teaching, professional and business work.

c) The third position sees headship in terms of marriage only. For the 'authority' which women are not to exercise over men in the Church (1 Timothy 2) seems to be *authentēs* (domineering and usurping authority) rather than *exousia* (the word usually used for authority) as evidenced by Paul's specific choice of the verb *authentein*. But this should present no problems, for this behaviour is forbidden those in the Church anyway. What should guide Christian behaviour at all times is humility and love. What is more, even within marriage 'headship' no longer means 'exercising authority'. For the only time when men are asked to exercise authority (*exousia*) over their wives is in the sexual sense (1 Corinthians 11) but here of course it is made mutual: the wife is also to have authority over her husband's body. What is more, being a 'helpmeet' does not mean in the Hebrew (*ezer,* Genesis 2) being a 'subordinate', but an equal. If headship does not mean holding authority over, what then does it mean? The answer comes in the analogy of Ephesians 5 with Christ and the Church. For headship means men loving their wives as Christ loved the Church, that is with sacrificial, self-denying love. The example of Christ's relationship with the Church is of that of a servant: he came not to be ministered to, but to minister. The essence of headship is therefore *servanthood.* For the word 'head' is used in this sense of source and has little to do with authority. Nor does Paul ask wives to *obey* husbands. The word now translated 'submit' *hupotasso* (Ephesians 5, Colossians 3.18) is very different from 'obey' (Colossians 3. 20, 22, children and slaves), and involves a much more voluntary act.

d)   A fourth position sees the whole teaching of headship as within a culturally changing context. The key to understanding the instructions given in Ephesians 5, Titus 2 and Colossians 3 is not that of some divinely constituted permanent hierarchy, but that of the unity of the body of Christ. Within the New Testament Church were very diverse groups and many different status groupings: noblemen, paupers, children, old people, Greeks, Jews, slaves, slave-owners, men and women. Two issues preoccupied Paul: that the unity of the whole body be preserved, and that unbelievers outside should not be caused to stumble. For this reason he took the element which was most likely to be abused in these sets of relationships and stressed that. So the need for husbands to *love,* for slave-owners to be *lenient and just,* for wives to be *respectful* and *non-aggressive* (submissive), for slaves to be *obedient.* But this no more meant that Paul was instilling a male — dominant, female — subordinate hierarchy than it meant he was endorsing slavery. He was stressing what the proprieties were in those situations. In fact the key to understanding the deeper relationship was not in those passages at all but in Ephesians 5. 21 where he tells everyone to submit to one another out of reverence for Christ, and in Galatians 3.28 where he insists that in Christ 'there is neither Jew nor Greek, slave nor free, male nor female, for you are all one in Christ Jesus'.

It should not be worrying that there is this variety of positions held by committed Christians. Nor is it surprising that those who hold either of the first two positions are usually the ones who feel theirs alone is biblical. And yet the weight of the evidence seems to me to be against them. Nowhere does Christ himself put forward an authoritative hierarchical model: he rebukes his disciples severely for trying to move into one. Since Paul also endorses both Christ's example and the absence of any divisions at the deepest level it is clear that we need a new framework for understanding some of the passages. Paul also clearly approves of very non-subordinate activities of many women, and balances his own comments on women being silent (1 Timothy 2) with full approbation of women praying and prophesying (1 Corinthians 11). What is certainly the case is that the issue is by no means as clear cut as those who hold the hierarchical view would want to maintain.

Index

184